Equitable Access

Information and Communication Technology For Open and Distance Learning

Olivia A. T. Frimpong Kwapong

iUniverse, Inc.
New York Bloomington

iUniverse books may be ordered through booksellers or by contacting:

iUniverse
1663 Liberty Drive
Bloomington, IN 47403
www.iuniverse.com
1-800-Authors (1-800-288-4677)

ISBN: 978-1-4401-9417-7 (sc)
ISBN: 978-1-4401-9418-4 (ebook)
ISBN: 978-1-4401-9420-7 (dj)

Printed in the United States of America

Contents

initiatives around the globe to apply ICT to address issues of poverty in developing countries. ICTs are applicable to all sectors, most especially education, livelihoods, health care, and government, which are directly linked to poverty alleviation. Five of the eight Millennium Development Goals (MDGs) focus on these sectors, which attract a lot of attention in discussions on ICT and poverty alleviation.

Ghana has set a goal of achieving middle-income status by the year 2020 (Vision 2020). This vision is embedded in the country's MDGs and its Poverty Reduction Strategy Program (PRSP I&II) (Ghana 2003b; 2006). There are strong indications that Ghana will be able to meet the MDGs with effective policies that target poverty alleviation. The real gross domestic product growth has averaged about 5 percent since 1983, and overall poverty declined from 52 percent in 1992 to 28 percent in 2006 (World Bank 2007; 2008). Although the debate on appropriate strategies to push the development agenda has focused on the availability of the traditional factors of production—land, labor, and capital—there is an emerging consensus that the efficient use of information and communication technology could be indispensable to any credible effort to turn the corner toward higher levels of growth and improvement in the human condition (Kwapong 2009abc). Professor Allotey first raised the alarm, saying, "We paid the price of not taking part in the Industrial Revolution … because we did not have the opportunity to see what was taking place in Europe. Now we see that information and communication technology (ICT) has become an indispensable tool. This time we should not miss out on this technological revolution" (Allotey in Opoku 2004).

Information and communication technologies can be interpreted broadly as technologies that facilitate communication and the processing and transmission of information by electronic means. This definition encompasses the full range of ICTs, from radio and television to telephones (fixed and mobile), computers, and the Internet (UNESCO 2003). The core of the country's development agenda is poverty alleviation and improvement in the socioeconomic well-being of people in rural and urban areas. With improvements in ICT, it is possible to design and manage a policy that makes it possible to introduce information to education and empower the strategic groups in the rural and urban areas. The government recognizes this opportunity and has succinctly stated that "Ghana's ICT development goal is to develop an ICT-driven socio-economic development policy and plan that will aid Ghana's developmental effort and move the economy and society towards a knowledge-based information society and economy in the shortest possible time" (Ghana 2004).

The government of Ghana recognizes the need for extensive human capital development to achieve the objective of poverty alleviation in the country. This is especially true in the context of training people in tertiary institutions to lead the economic development agenda. However, as a result of limited space and a mismatch between the qualified applicants and existing facilities, a high percentage of qualified applicants do not gain admission to existing universities to pursue further studies. Available statistics indicate that from 1996 to 2001, on average only about 32 percent of qualified applicants for admission into the universities and about 54 percent of same for admission into the polytechnics were actually admitted. The figures have not changed much since. For the 2005/2006 academic year, 55 percent of qualified applicants were admitted into all the public universities and 78 percent into the polytechnics. For the same period, statistics indicate that although the male-female enrollment for both the universities and polytechnics has increased slightly, the gap between men and women is still very wide. In the 2005/2006 academic year the male-to-female enrollment ratio was 65:35 for the universities and 70:30 for the polytechnics. This is far below the national norm of 50 percent males to 50 percent females (NCTE 2006). The disparity begins at the secondary school level and continues through the tertiary level. Statistics on basic and secondary education indicate that only about 30 percent of junior high school (JHS) graduates are able to gain admission to senior high school (SHS), and only about 35 percent of SHS graduates are able to gain admission to universities and polytechnics, plus another 10–20 percent to diploma-level postsecondary education. There are not many private secondary schools, so they are able to enroll only a minimal number of qualified applicants. It has been noted that at the tertiary level about 5,000 undergraduates are enrolled in secular degree-granting programs in the existing nine private institutions (Ghana n.d.; NCTE 2006).

In response to the situation, the government of Ghana has long explored the need to use distance learning to respond to the educational needs of the large number of qualified applicants, especially at the tertiary level, who do not have access to education because of space limitations or because they are in remote regions of the country. This is highly emphasized in the country's most recent educational policy, in which the government seeks to establish an open university and set up community open colleges in all the regions (Ghana 2004).

A distance education (DE) policy of the Ministry of Education outlines that programs be provided to

- increase access to and participation in education of all types and at all levels for all;
- facilitate progression through the education system;
- improve people's capacity to cope with rapid changes in knowledge and skills and thereby improve upon their contribution to the economy and society;
- increase equality and democratization of education; and

- make education cost-effective and affordable (Mensah and Owusu-Mensah 2002).

Currently four of the public universities—University of Ghana (UG), University of Cape Coast (UCC), Kwame Nkrumah University of Science and Technology (KNUST), and University of Education, Winneba (UEW)—are offering their academic programs in a dual mode. The programs are being patronized greatly by both males and females in the country, and characteristic of most distance learning institutions, the percentage of female enrollment cannot compare with that of on-campus programs. For instance, statistics of the various institutions indicate that UEW, which began in 1998, has approximately 7,000 students, with 53 percent females and 46.5 percent males at its Level 300 for the 2006/2007 school year; UCC, which began in 2001, has more than 18,000 students, 49.7 percent females and 50.2 percent males in the Diploma in Education courses (Kwapong 2007b). Facilities such as libraries in the existing universities are already overstretched because of the large number of students.

The distance education programs that are being offered are mainly print-based, supported with occasional face-to-face interaction where students meet their tutors at a center for discussions. Assignments are either hand delivered or mailed by post. Students meet at a designated center to write their end-of-semester examinations. In cases where course materials are not ready, lecturers either meet to lecture the students in the various centers or students join the on-campus lectures. Distance education students also share the already overstretched facilities such as libraries with the on-campus students. Meanwhile the purpose is to use distance education to decongest the various campuses. Allowing DE students to share libraries, attend lectures, and share other on-campus facilities will no doubt congest the system further. Much as these educational processes create opportunity for those who will otherwise not gain admission to pursue their life's dream of education, it presents enormous challenges to the DE institutions and most especially learners from remote parts of the country. Traveling to centers for tutorials or lectures will not only expose learners and students to the risks of highway robbery and accident but also may not be cost-effective for the institution and the student as well. Considering ODL as a mode that meets women's lifestyle needs because they can conveniently work, keep their homes, and study, excessive use of face-to-face interactions may not work well for them. For some women, obtaining permission from their husbands to attend tutorials or other academic programs could be more challenging than obtaining permission from the workplace (Kwapong 2008a). A continuation of such practices may make the program lose its distance-learning philosophy and turn into a face-to-face program instead. In this case learners may be forced to leave their jobs more often and those who cannot afford to leave the workplace or cannot obtain permission may drop out of the program.

These are challenges that most countries, especially those in the developed world, have used ICT to overcome. The rapid advancement in information technology has dictated the pace of growth of correspondence education into distance education and now online learning, e-learning, and virtual university or technology-mediated learning. With technological advancement, the *distance* and *isolation* in the distance learning system has been overcome to a very large extent. Available data show that technologies in Ghana have been estimated to be 356,400 telephone lines, 5,207 mobile cellular phones, zero AM, 49 FM, and three shortwave radio broadcast stations, and seven television broadcast stations. It is estimated that 2,899 Internet hosts could now join in the information transfer for 609,800 Internet users (Infoplease n.d.; Ghana n.d.; Ghana 2003a). With conscious policy directives, the available basic ICT resources could be used to improve the delivery of the existing open and distance learning programs. It is in this vein that the book seeks to explore the potential of ICT tools for supporting the distance learning program to facilitate equitable access to tertiary education with particular reference to Ghana.

Acknowledgments

I remain grateful to all those who have contributed in diverse ways to the publication of this book, most especially the Rockefeller Foundation for the one-month residency at Bellagio Study Center, Italy.

Dedication

To My Daughter,

Theodoxea

Part 1 Education and ICT in Ghana

Chapter 1

Education in Ghana: A Contextual Overview

Background

Ghana's formal educational system has gone through several phases of reform to identify an educational system that responds to the times as well as national aspirations. In most cases, the reforms have dealt with content, methods, or duration. During the missionary and colonial era, education focused on transformation of the individual to suit the Western lifestyle, particularly in the areas of religion and occupation.

The traditional notion of education is the type of teaching and learning that occurs in personal contact between the teacher and the learner in the classroom setting. This is anchored in the reality that teaching and learning take place at the same time and same place. With the introduction of new technology, including printed materials for correspondence, it became clear that formal, informal, or non-formal teaching and learning could also be done via technology. The rapid development in learning theories and advancement in technology has made it possible to shift from institution-led learning to own-time self-learning at a distance. Thus the trend has moved from face-to-face teaching to self-paced learning, which is gradually moving toward flexibility and openness. It is this experience that has progressed to the alternative delivery system known as the ODL system (Infoplease n.d.)

The views on the use of ICT for teaching and learning and sustainable development in the developing world are divergent. There has been the argument that developing countries should focus on more immediate and pressing needs such as jobs, food, water, education, and electricity instead of ICT for development and education, which requires considerable expenditure of scarce resources (Gulati 2008). Others have responded in support of a full exploration of the use of ICT as a tool for attacking the difficult problem of poverty alleviation (Abdulkafi 2008; Robinson 2008). For most scholars and policy leaders, ICT is one of the contributing factors to social and economic disparities across different social and economic groups, disparities between developed and developing countries, between rural and urban dwellers, between men and women, and between the elite and the illiterate. Hence the need to explore its potential to bridge the various divides through education (Opoku 2004).

Educational Reforms in Ghana

After independence, Ghana continued to search for a system of education that was relevant to the world of work and adequate for rural development and the modernization of its agriculture-based economy. The country has also been interested in a system of education that seeks to promote national and cultural identity and citizenship.

Some of the laws, policy documents, and reports that have been adopted over the years by the various governments for meeting the educational needs and aspirations of the people include the following:

- Accelerated Development Plan for Education, 1951

- Education Act of 1961 (Act 87)
- Dzobo Report of 1973 (recommended the Junior Secondary School/Senior Secondary School concept)
- New Structure and Content of Education 1974
- Ghana Education Service Decree 1974
- Education Commission Report on Basic and Secondary Education 1987/88
- Education Reform Program 1987/88
- University Relationalization Committee Report 1988
- Constitution of the Republic of Ghana 1992
- Ghana Education Service Act of 1995
- Free Compulsory Universal Basic Education Program, 1996 (1992 Constitution)
- FCUBE Policy Document and Program of Operations, 1996
- Ghana Education Trust Fund—GET Fund Act 2000 (Act 581)
- Ghana Vision 2020 document
- Review of Education Reforms in Ghana 2002
- White Paper Report on Education Reform Review 2004

These initiatives have contributed to structural transformation of the educational system in improving access, high-quality teaching, and learning. Infrastructural delivery as well as management efficiency has also been improved. There have, however, been some identifiable weaknesses that have led to the various reviews in the educational system. For instance, much as President Nkrumah's Accelerated Development Plan of Education contributed to the expansion of enrollment in elementary and secondary education in the country, it also affected the standard of education at the basic and secondary levels and produced a lot of unemployed school leavers. The policy was also popularly described as too elitist. The implementation of the Dzobo Report of 1973 in the year 1987 made a tremendous impact on the system of education of the country by introducing the Junior Secondary School (JSS) system for teaching both academic and practical skills. After more than twenty years of practice, the assessment report revealed that the system had produced a large number of older teenage school leavers, most of whom were deficient in basic math and literacy skills. Graduates of the JSS level had also been described as ill-prepared for either formal second-cycle education or the life of work and lifelong learning for self-actualization (Ghana 2004; Ghana 2007a; Ghana 2003a).

The Current Review of Education

Recognizing the drawbacks in previous educational reforms, a committee was set up in 2002 to review the entire educational system to make it more responsive to current challenges. The task of the committee focused on an examination of the structure of education, issues affecting development and delivery of education, the constrained access to different levels of the educational ladder, information and communication technology application, and distance education, among others.

Based on the report of the committee, the country decided to settle on a philosophy of education that seeks to create well-balanced, all-around people with adequate knowledge, skills, values, aptitudes, and attitudes to become functional and productive citizens. The underlying principle is that as the human resource of a country that has a great economic ambition, Ghanaians should be trained to become enterprising and develop the capability of responding to the demands of a fast-changing world that is driven by science and technology (Ghana 2002; 2004).

Highlighting the philosophy of independent learning, the committee has provided foundational principles of education that emphasize learning in which learners take an active role instead of teaching that is dominated by the teacher. There is the call for focus on continuous lifelong learning instead of a one-shot formal school experience. Quality of access to education for all has been listed as one of the foundational principles as well.

In this case, one does not continue to see education as having an end but rather as a process and a way of life that forms part of life till death. The idea of independent learning in which the learner takes an active role is also remarkable. By this, the country is moving for a lifelong and learner-centered approach to education that is more empowering compared with the historical perception of a short-term and teacher-centered approach.

Based on the review, Ghana's education goals have been incorporated into the ten policy goals of the Education Strategic Plan, 2003–15, as follows:

1. Increase access to and participation in education and training

2. Improve quality of teaching and learning for enhanced pupil/student achievement
3. Extend and improve technical and vocational education and training
4. Promote good health and environmental sanitation in schools and institutions of higher learning
5. Strengthen and improve educational planning and management
6. Promote and extend the provision of science and technology education and training
7. Improve the quality of academic and research programs
8. Promote and extend preschool education
9. Identify and promote education programs that will assist in the prevention and management of HIV/AIDS
10. Provide girls with equal opportunities to access the full cycle of education

The idea of widening access to education, promoting independent and lifelong learning, and adopting alternative approaches to delivery of education is prominent in the outlined goals of education.

Snapshots of the New Educational Policy

The results from the 2002 Education Review and the government's white paper on the review of new educational reforms that took effect in the 2007/2008 academic year have introduced some structural changes that have affected content, delivery, and duration of education in the country. The following are highlights of the educational reforms as provided by the Ministry of Education, Science and Sports (MOESS 2008).

General

- Universal and continuous basic educational program for eleven years from age four to fifteen, made up of
  - two years of kindergarten,
  - six years of primary school, and
  - three years of junior high school (JHS).
- The medium of instruction in kindergarten and lower primary school will be in the Ghanaian language and English, where necessary.
- At the basic level, emphasis shall be on literacy, math, creative arts, and problem-solving skills.
- The JHS will be followed by a four-year senior high school (SHS) system where students may choose to go into different streams comprising general education and technical, vocational, and education training (TVET), or enter into an apprenticeship scheme. Government will take full responsibility for the first year of a structured apprenticeship system for JHS leavers.
- A new four-year SHS will offer general education with electives in general, business, technical, vocational, and agriculture options for entry into a tertiary institution or the job market.
- Technical, vocational, and agricultural institutions will offer four-year courses, including the core SHS subjects.
- Teacher-training colleges will be upgraded and conditions of service of teachers improved, with special incentives for teachers in rural areas.
- Metropolitan, Municipal, and District Assemblies shall be responsible for the infrastructure, supervision, and monitoring of basic and senior high schools.

- A new National Inspectorate Board outside the Ghana Education Service but under the MOESS shall be responsible for periodic inspection of basic and secondary schools to ensure quality education.
- Free Compulsory Universal Basic Education (FCUBE) and cost-sharing at the senior high and tertiary levels shall be maintained.
- Educational services will be widened to include library and information, guidance and counseling, and distance education.
- The private sector will be encouraged to increase its participation in the provision of educational services.
- Greater emphasis will be put on information and communication technology and science and technology.
- Special-needs education will be improved at all levels.

Curriculum

- At the kindergarten level, lessons will be learned through play, with emphasis on numeracy and creative arts.
- At the lower primary level, English, basic mathematical skills, natural science, and the dominant Ghanaian language of the area shall be taught.
- At the lower primary level, English and Ghanaian languages shall incorporate concepts of religious and moral education, science and hygiene, life skills, civics, and culture.
- At the upper primary level, subjects shall be the dominant Ghanaian language, English, basic mathematical skills, integrated science, and citizenship education.

- At the primary level, physical education, music, dance, and other creative arts shall be taught as practical subjects.
- At the junior high school, English; mathematics; social studies; integrated science including agricultural science; a Ghanaian language; technical, vocational, and agricultural education and training (pre-technical vocational); ICT; and French shall be taught.
- Guidance and counseling shall be offered to students at the JHS to enable them to choose the right courses to suit their interest and skills.
- After JHS, there will be two parallel streams made up of general education.
- At the senior high school (SHS), the core subjects shall be English, mathematics, integrated science, social studies, and ICT.
- In addition to the core subjects at the SHS, every student must select one of the following course programs: agriculture, business, technical, vocational, (home economics or visual arts), or general (arts or science).
- For the technical/vocational/agriculture education stream of SHS, the following broad elective areas shall be offered: building trades, business studies, electrical engineering, hospitality trades, mechanical engineering, and agriculture.
- Curriculum shall be developed to meet the needs of children and youth with special educational needs.

Teacher Education

- A National Teaching Council shall coordinate and regulate teacher education and training programs.
- Education-oriented universities shall be responsible for the certification of teachers.

- Untrained teachers in basic schools will have access to remedial courses through distance education.
- Continuous teacher development will be undertaken to upgrade and update the competencies and skills of serving teachers.
- Special attention will be given to the training of teachers in technical, vocational, agricultural, special-needs education, guidance and counseling, ICT, and French.
- Teacher-training programs for kindergarten teachers shall be developed.
- Conditions of service for teachers shall be improved.
- Open universities and distance learning colleges shall be established to train and retrain teachers.
- Curriculum on special-needs education in Teacher-training colleges shall be enhanced to ensure early identification and effective management of children with special educational needs.

Inspection of Schools

- There shall be an independent National Inspectorate Board to formulate, set, and enforce standards in all pre-tertiary schools.
- The board shall make recommendations to the minister on issues of quality assurance and set up mechanisms to enforce its recommendations.

Technical, Vocational, and Agricultural Education and Training (TVET)

- TVET shall provide employable skills through formal and informal apprenticeship; vocational, technical, and agricultural institutes; polytechnics; and universities.
- Pre-tertiary TVET shall be provided at the following levels: technical institutes, vocational institutes, and

apprenticeship (formal and informal). It shall also be offered as part of basic education and as elective subjects in secondary schools.

- There shall be two types of apprenticeship training regulated by the National Apprenticeship Training Board:
    - Formal scheme, to be made up of classroom and on-the-job training.
    - On-the-job training (informal) under traditional master craftspeople.
- The competency-based training curriculum delivery methodology has been adopted for the TVET system. In this approach strong emphasis will be placed on students acquiring practical skills for employment.
- The service conditions for TVET teachers shall be improved to attract qualified and experienced teachers from industry.
- TVET shall be resourced and promoted as a viable alternative to general education (MOESS 2007; Ghana 2004; Ghana 2002).

Of special interest to the focus of this book are the policies on distance education or open colleges and ICT and those that seek to increase access. To facilitate human resource development in the country and widen access to education at all levels to ensure equitable distribution of education, the new educational policy has emphasized the use of distance learning and information technologies. Distance learning for teacher education has proved useful for most developing countries to address teacher shortages. Supported with ICT, thousands of people from the remotest parts of their countries have been able to access education though distance learning (Spencer 1994; Swale 1999; Thomas 2001; Toure 2007; UNISA 2007; UNESCO 2004).

Following the philosophy of education in the country, the policy framework has been set up to train skilled Ghanaians who can develop the agricultural base and all other aspects of the economy. There are also policy guidelines to promote continuing education and lifelong learning through open and distance learning modes. In connection with global trends and the potential of ICTs to facilitate teaching and learning and productivity in the world of work, the Education Review Committee of Ghana had the responsibility of examining the use of ICT for distance learning at all levels of education in the country. Hence the recommendation that conscious effort be made to include ICT in the curricula at different levels and to fully use it in the delivery of education.

There is special mention in the policy document to establish open universities and open colleges and support distance education to create avenues for work and study programs and lifelong learning in general. This will also respond to the need for continuing education for the large number of Ghanaians who do not gain access to existing tertiary institutions.

The policy is not silent on ensuring gender equity in education. In partnership with the private sector and civic organizations, the policy seeks to address the issue of female dropouts at the various levels of education. The current focus of the policy of education in the Ghana has made distance education and the use of ICT in education very critical.

Chapter 2

Education in Ghana: Access and Equity Issues

"Education for all" was originally proposed by Confucius as the ideal of education for all societies (Lee 2004). Education for all simply means all students have equal access to high-quality education. Provision of access and equity in education has since received policy lines in both national and international development agendas. This is based on the principle that to obtain a more equitable society, all individuals should ideally have access to equivalent learning opportunities, regardless of their socioeconomic background, social origin, age, or gender. Equity of access provides a strong base for developing social cohesion (OECD 2004; Ampah 2009).

The constitution of the Republic of Ghana, Article 38 requires government to provide access to Free Compulsory Universal Basic Education (FCUBE) and, depending on resource availability, to senior secondary, technical, and tertiary education and lifelong learning. This constitutional provision has guided the provision of education by various governments in spite of the numerous challenges that emerge. This chapter will focus on the state of provision of equitable access to education in Ghana at all levels and in all special programs and its implications for ICT use for open and distance learning.

Access and Equity in Education

Generally access to education refers to the ability to get entry into educational institutions. Improving access could therefore include creating more opportunities for education and overcoming all the barriers to education such as improving physical access to a training venue for the sake of those with disabilities and ensuring that selection criteria do not discriminate against prospective applicants based on race or gender. This usually calls for expansion of human and material educational resources and the use of marketing activities to encourage all qualified applicants. Access issues form a subset within equity issues (CAPA n.d.; Chen and Chen 2008; Considine, Watson, and Hall 2005).

Equity in education is viewed as the extent to which individuals can take advantage of education and training, in terms of opportunities, access, treatment, and outcomes. It is just about the ideal that guarantees all students, regardless of race, national origin, gender, religion, physical disability, or special needs, equal opportunities in education.

Equitable systems ensure that the outcomes of education and training are independent of socioeconomic background and other factors that lead to educational disadvantage and that treatment reflects individuals' specific learning needs. Equity issues thus range from providing a supportive learning environment to adjusting assessments to meet individual circumstances, from policies on fee reduction to development of inclusive training materials. Basically, equity refers to the ability to achieve results in training and to receive training in an inclusive environment with inclusive materials (Commission of the European Communities 2006; Vetinfonet n.d.; Jefferson 2007; Dassin n.d.; Dikshit, Garg, Panda, and Vijayshri 2002).

In other words, equity is about ensuring that all people and all groups of people participate, have the opportunity to reach their potential, make choices, and receive responsive and appropriate products and services. Thus the destination for all learners is the same, but the journey may be different. For example, some learners may gain qualifications through an access course process; others may complete a training program before being assessed; some may have to go through an access program before entry and be assessed at the end of program as well; some learners may also need more time than others because of family responsibilities or because they are returning to learning after a long interval (Cookson 2002; Kasday 2001; Yiwan and Wei 2008).

Access and equity policy could then be based on the following tenets:

- Delivering and maintaining training services that reflect fair and reasonable opportunity, and consideration for all students and staff, regardless of race, color, religion, gender, physical disability, or the prevailing community values
- Equity for all people through the fair and appropriate allocation of resources
- Equality of outcome in education for all people, without discrimination
- Access for all people to appropriate quality education and training programs and services
- Increased opportunity for people to participate in vocational and technical education and other poorly patronized training programs and their related decision-making processes (Kasday and Noble 2000)
- Kasday and Noble have noted that it could be misleading to think of equity as referring to gender. There are various aspects of equity. These include gender-related equity, income-related equity, region-

related equity, religion-related equity, physical ability–related equity, and socio-cultural–related equity.

- *Gender-related equity* refers to the opportunities of the traditionally disadvantaged gender group, females, in their access to various levels of education, opportunities for success in education, and opportunities to make use of education as an asset for enhancing their life chances.
- *Income-related equity* concerns financially disadvantaged groups, such as the income poor, in their access to various levels of education and their opportunities for success in education. Imbalances in economic levels have created a wide gap in education access and quality between rich urban areas and the poor rural areas in most communities of developing nations.
- *Region-related equity* is about the educational opportunities of the people living in disadvantaged regions or localities. In most cases, the disadvantaged regions are rural, but they can also be economically backward regions within an economy or the income poor within urban areas.
- *Religion-related equity* deals with barriers that emerge from beliefs and practices of some groups of people based on religion that affects their full access to education.
- *Physical ability–related equity* looks at people with physical challenges and their inability to access education. Most infrastructures in educational institutes, modes of delivery, resources, facilities, and some services are not often accessible to some people because of their physical challenges.
- *Socio-cultural–related equity* deals with the educational opportunities of socio-culturally

disadvantaged groups. In most cases, they are ethnic minorities within the economy, but sometimes women are also regarded as minorities in certain respects, and their educational opportunities are limited by socio-cultural perceptions of women that are unfavorable for them to receive education.

Dealing with the various aspects of equity in education serves as a response to international declarations of education and human rights. Article 3 of the 1990 World Declaration on Education for All stated that "basic education should be provided to all children, youth, and adults." This is reemphasized in the following six goals of Education for All during the Dakar conference in 2000:

Goal 1: expanding and improving comprehensive early childhood care and education, especially for the most vulnerable and disadvantaged children

Goal 2: ensuring that by 2015 all children, particularly girls, children in difficult circumstances, and those belonging to ethnic minorities, have access to and complete free and compulsory primary education of good quality

Goal 3: ensuring that the learning needs of all young people and adults are met through equitable access to appropriate learning and life skills programs

Goal 4: achieving a 50 percent improvement in levels of adult literacy by 2015, especially for women, and equitable access to basic and continuing education for all adults

Goal 5: eliminating gender disparities in primary and secondary education by 2005, and achieving gender equality in education by 2015, with a focus on ensuring girls' full and equal access to and achievement in basic education of good quality

Goal 6: improving all aspects of the quality of education and ensuring excellence of all, so that recognized and measurable learning outcomes are achieved by all, especially in literacy, numeracy, and essential life skills (UNESCO 2000; UNESCO 2006; Lee 2004)

To ensure that there is equitable distribution of basic education, all children, youth, and adults must be given the opportunity to achieve and maintain an acceptable level of learning. This should not just be targeting basic education but should focus on widening access to education at all levels for all categories of people in society. It is still necessary to give urgent priority to ensure access to, and improve the quality of, education for girls and women, and to remove every obstacle and stereotyping that hampers their active participation in education at all levels. Essentially, underserved groups, such as the poor; street and working children; rural and remote populations; nomads and migrant workers; indigenous peoples; ethnic, racial, and linguistic minorities; refugees; those displaced by war; and people under occupation, should not suffer any discrimination in access to education irrespective of the content and level (Kasozi n.d.; UMPA 2003; King 2006; Kurubacak 2002; Nagel n.d.; UNESCO 2008; Remer 2008; Rumble 2008; Tripathi and Mukerji 2008).

Issues of Access and Equity in Education in Ghana

Against the backdrop of the need to promote equitable access to education for all at all levels, educational policies of Ghana have focused on making education equitably distributed across regions, sex, income, and religion. The mission of the Ministry of Education is "to provide relevant education to all Ghanaians at all levels to enable them acquire skills that will assist them to develop their potential, be productive, facilitate poverty reduction and promote socio-economic growth and national development" (MEOSS 2007; Ghana n.d.; Ghana 2002; Ghanaweb n.d.).

In fulfilment of their mission to provide equitable access to education for all, the Ministry of Education has set goals to provide the following:

- facilities to ensure that all citizens, irrespective of age, gender, tribe, religion, and political affiliation, are functionally literate and self-reliant
- basic education for all
- opportunities for open education for all
- education and training for skill development with emphasis on science, technology, and creativity
- higher education for the development of middle and top-level manpower requirements
- resources that will give girls equal opportunities to access the full cycle of education

These goals have directed the drawing up of the Education Strategic Plan, which seeks to assist in the poverty reduction process through the development of a learning society to enhance human resources in the country. The plan anticipates meaningful and successful participation in the education process for both young people and adults who have hitherto been excluded. In the process such people will be able to access new opportunities for educational development. The strategic plan is further designed to ensure that all learners gain the necessary knowledge, master the necessary skills, and acquire the necessary attitudes for them to develop as individuals, and to improve their social well-being and Ghanaian society as well.

As a strategy for increasing access to and participation in education and training, the plan has been drawn up to provide a foundation for increased educational attainment through the development of access to free compulsory universal basic education (FCUBE), promoting the enrollment of girls and other disadvantaged groups, and by increasing opportunities for out-of-school and hard-to-reach children and adults. In addition, the plan seeks to expand access to the secondary and tertiary subsectors, including the polytechnics, and to establish an open university.

In providing access to females for achieving gender equity, the plan specifically seeks to provide girls with equal opportunities to access the full cycle of education. The Ministry of Education has set up strategies in the plan to increase female participation in the education sector, in terms of enrollments, retention, and completion rates. Specific strategies for achieving the set target include sensitization programs, highlighting the importance of female education, and other programs to support female access to education at all levels.

The Current Situation

The country is currently going through educational reform to make its education more accessible and equitable. Available records show that Ghana has 12,130 primary schools, 5,450 Junior Secondary Schools, 503 senior secondary schools, 18 technical institutions, 38 training colleges, 7 theological colleges, 8 tutorial colleges, 10 polytechnics, and 6 public and 13 private universities that serve a population of about 20 million. Figure 1 provides the details. Total school enrollment is estimated at almost 2 million, with a breakdown of 1.3 million primary, 107,600 secondary, 21,280 technical, 11,300 teacher training, and 5,600 university (Ghana 2007ab; MOESS 2009). Compared with the number of schools that the country had at the time of independence in 1957 (one university and a handful of secondary and primary schools) one will observe from the current developments that access to education has increased. As a result most Ghanaians could have relatively easy access to education. But one can clearly see that the increment does not match the growing population and their demand for education at all levels.

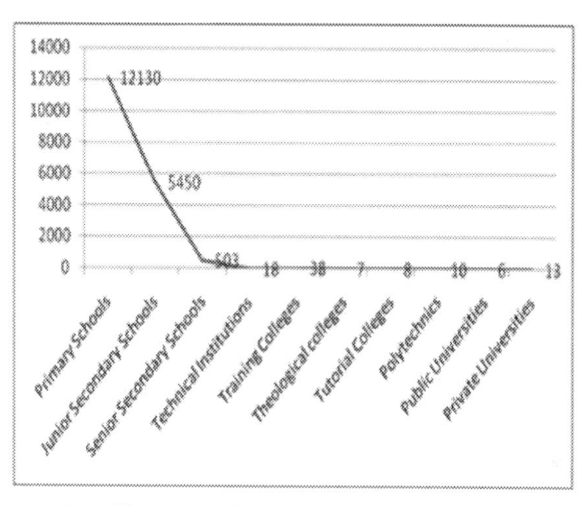

Figure 1 Current Status of Education in Ghana

Basic Education

The basic education provision in Ghana is to ensure quality basic education for all children of school-going age irrespective of gender and geographical location. In the FCUBE policy the basic education system is supposed to provide access to and participation in basic education for all children of school-going age. In light of the policy, the Basic Education Division is responsible for increasing access and retention, and ensuring continuous schooling within a nine-year basic education period for all children of school-going age. The division also ensures good-quality teaching and learning outcomes in all basic schools and equity in the distribution of teaching and learning materials, including infrastructure.

Tables 1, 2, and 3 and Figures 2, 3, and 4 indicate growth in enrollment for both males and females at the primary and JHS levels over the seven-year period. This could imply that the country has been doing well in making education accessible. A closer look at the data in Table 3, however, will reveal that the gross enrollment ratio (GER) for both males and females at primary and JHS levels has not reached 100 percent. That of the girls has been consistently lower than that of the boys. The GER for boys in primary school in the 2007/2008 school year is 97.1 percent, whereas that of girls is 92.8 percent. At the JHS level for the same year, the GER for boys is at 82.2 percent and that of girls is 75.2 percent. A similar trend emerges in the GER of deprived districts in the country. However, comparing the percentage from 2003 to 2007 one will see an appreciable increase from 70.1 percent to 91.2 percent.

Overall progress in the GER at the primary level is more encouraging than at the JHS level for both sexes. The drop at the JHS level is not appreciable. It is just too early for pupils to be dropping out of school at that quantum. This is more critical when one looks at statistics on completion rate at the primary and JHS levels in Table 4. With a current (2007/2008) male percentage of 88 and female percentage of 82.3 at the primary level, the rate drops to 72.3 percent for males and 62.8 percent for females at the JHS level. Completion rate for boys has also been consistently higher than that of girls at both the primary and JHS levels.

Table 1 Enrollment in Primary Schools

Enrollment	2001/2002	2002/2003	2003/2004	2004/2005	2005/2006	2006/2007	2007/2008
Girls	1,227,284	1,201,067	1,262,220	1,403,988	1,516,725	1,633,600	1,755,734
Boys	1,359,150	1,323,518	1,403,913	1,525,548	1,606,178	1,732,162	1,860,289
Total	2,586,434	2,524,585	2,686,133	2,929,536	3,122,903	3,365,762	3,616,023
% Girls	47.5	47.6	47.7	47.9	48.6	48.5	48.6

Source: MOESS 20

Table 1 Enrollment in Primary Schools

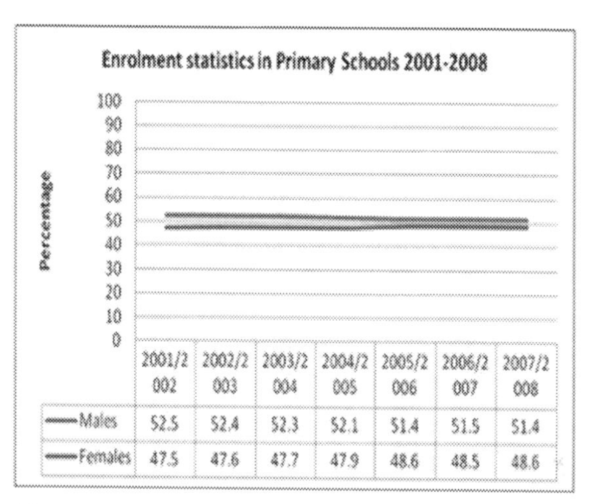

Figure 2 Enrollment in Primary Schools

Table 2 Enrollments in Junior High Schools (JHS)

Enrollment	2001/2002	2002/2003	2003/2004	2004/2005	2005/2006	2006/2007	2007/2008
Girls	397,122	396,299	420,548	462,090	483,741	527,232	571,864
Boys	468,514	468,934	498,786	548,156	557,261	605,086	652,146
Total	865,636	865,233	919,334	1,010,246	1,041,002	1,132,318	1,224,010
% Girls	45.9	45.8	45.7	45.7	46.5	46.6	46.7

Source: MOESS 2008

Table 2 Enrollments in Junior High Schools (JHS)

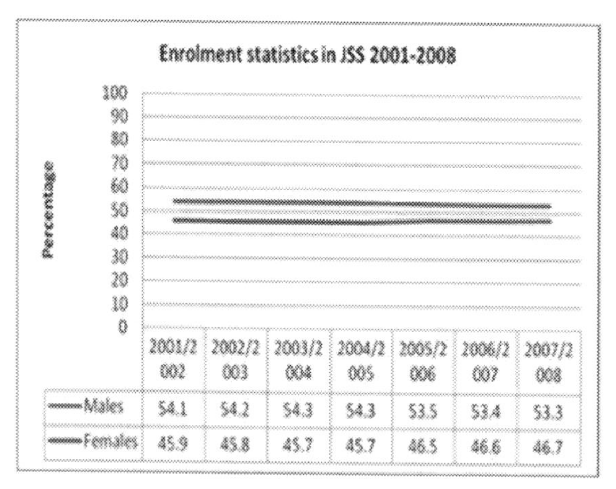

Figure 3 Enrollments in Junior High Schools

Table 3 Gross Enrollment Ratio for Primary and JHS

GER	2002/2003		2003/2004		2004/2005		2005/2006		2006/2007		2007/2008	
PRIM—Total	75.7		78.4		83.3		86.4		90.8		95.0	
PRIM—M/F	M	F	M	F	M	F	M	F	M	F	M	F
	78.8	72.5	81.4	75.3	86.2	80.3	88.3	84.4	92.8	88.7	97.1	92.8
JHS —Total	63.4		65.6		70.2		70.4		74.8		78.8	
JHS—M/F	M	F	M	F	M	F 65.6	M	F	M	F 71.2	M	F
	67.3	59.3	69.7	61.3	74.6		73.8	66.9	78.3		82.2	75.2

Source: MOESS 2008

Table 3 Gross Enrollment Ratio for Primary and JHS

Table 4 Completion Rate for Primary and JHS

	2003/2004	2004/2005	2005/2006	2006/2007	2007/2008
PRIM	77.9	78.72	75.6	85.39	85.5
					M:88.7/F:82.3
JHS	58	60	77.9	64.95	67.7
					M:72.3/F:62.8

Source: MOESS 2008

Table 4 Completion Rate for Primary and JHS

Secondary Education

Secondary education is set up to provide Ghanaian children access to quality secondary education that will equip them with diverse skills, qualities, and attitudes that together form a sound basis for national socioeconomic development. Specifically the system seeks to reinforce and build on knowledge, skills, and attitudes acquired at the junior high school level, and to diversify the curriculum to cater to different talents and abilities. Secondary education in Ghana is also supposed to produce well-developed and productive individuals equipped with the qualities of responsible leadership, capable of fitting into a scientific and technological world and able to contribute to the development of their communities and the country as a whole.

Several interventions have been undertaken by government to improve the quality of secondary education all over the country and widen access as well. Government has been undertaking a model school project. The purpose of the model school project is to serve as a measure to respond to the increase in population coupled with the desire of parents to enroll their wards in well-established schools. The project is also to help increase access to quality secondary education across the country. The project is to upgrade one school in each district to a model status. Since 2003, when the first phase of the model schools started, thirty-one schools have benefited from the project. The African Development Bank is also funding the refurbishment and upgrading of twenty-five senior secondary schools throughout the country.

The New Partnership for Africa's Development's e-schools is also being undertaken to ensure that the youth of Africa will graduate from primary and secondary schools with skills that will enable them to participate effectively in the information society and knowledge economy. Specifically the e-school project aims at

- providing ICT skills and knowledge to primary and secondary school students; and
- providing teachers with ICT skills to enable them to use them as tools to enhance teaching and learning.

In Ghana, six schools (two urban, four rural) have been selected for the demonstration project.

These efforts to provide equitable access to secondary education have shown improvement in the enrollment of students. Statistics from 1989 to date (Table 5; Figure 4) shows that the number of secondary schools and enrollment have more than doubled from 250 to 646 schools and a total enrollment of 168,000 in 1989 to 437,771 in 2008. Meanwhile over the years, the female enrollment percentage has never reached the projected 50 percent target. Statistics for 2007/2008 show that the percentage share of girls' enrollment is 42.5 percent in public senior high schools, and in private schools, the figure was 54.4 percent in 2007/2008. The share of girls' enrollment in both public and private senior high schools was 43.7 percent in 2007/2008, an increase of 15.2 percent compared with the figure for 2006/2007.

Table 5 Enrollment Statistics (1990–2008)

Year	No. of Schools	Enrollment			
		Boys	Girls	Total	% Girls
1989/1990	250	112,542	55,458	168,000	33
1990/1991	404	133,581	65,679	199,000	33
1991/1992	413	150,740	74,537	225,277	33.1
1992/1993	438	164,623	82,873	247,496	33.5
1993/1994	452	154,927	81,603	253,530	32.2
1994/1995	452	130,446	71,367	201,813	35.4
1995/1996	453	122,070	72,015	194,085	37.1
1996/1997	455	115,881	73,027	188,908	38.7
1997/1998	464	118,033	74,383	192,416	38.7
1998/1999	464	121,588	76,624	198,212	38.7
1999/2000	464	117,275	87,351	204,626	42.7
2000/2001	474	132,786	99,309	232,095	42.8
2001/2002	474	143,245	106,747	249,992	42.7
2002/2003	476	172,536	128,770	301,306	42.7
2003/2004	476	189,479	143,642	333,121	43.1
2004/2005	485	201,717	159,783	361,500	44.2
2005/2006	485	236,409	187,263	423,672	44.2
2006/2007	539	—	—	414,491	—
2007/2008	646	246,646	191,125	437,771	43.7

Source: MOESS 2008

Table 5 Enrollment Statistics (1990–2008)

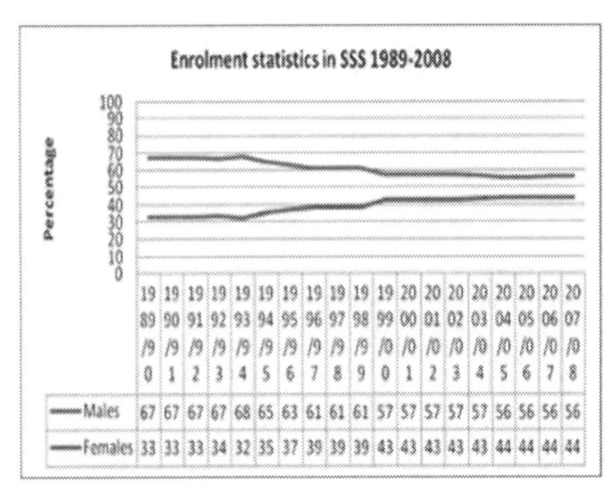

Figure 4 Enrollment Statistics (1990–2008)

Technical and Vocational Education Training (TVET)

TVET is provided in the country to offer relevant quality technical and vocational education and training skills delivery to meet Ghana's technical human resource requirements. In meeting this goal a division has been set up at the MOESS to

- assist in exposing students at the basic and SHS levels to a range of practical activities to make them familiar with and stimulate their interest in TVET programs so as to give them the opportunity to choose their future careers in the technical, vocational, or general education field;
- equip students who have completed basic education with TVET skills that will enable them to enter into gainful employment in the industry;
- equip students with relevant productive and entrepreneurial skills related to TVET courses that will prepare them for self-employment;
- promote increased participation of women in education, training, and employment in the TVET sector; and
- provide a sound academic foundation for TVET delivery and for further education for those students who may wish to continue their education during their working life in the context of lifelong education.

Generally TVET has been an area with low patronage in the country. Table 6 shows the trend of enrollment from 2002 to 2007. There has not been a stable increase in enrollment in TVET. The most current figure, 18,005 for the 2006/2007 school year, is below the figure of 19,777 for the 2002/2003 school year. This statistic has been reflected mostly in the enrollment for males, whereas that of females has steadily increased over the period. Meanwhile the total enrollment for females is less than a quarter that of men. What could be the reason for inconsistent enrollment in TVET programs? Why do females form such a low percentage? What factors should be put in place to make technical and vocational education equitably accessible? What teaching-learning media could be responsive to the learning styles of both sexes in TVET programs? These are some of the questions that come to mind for rethinking the TVET program in the country.

Table 6 Enrollment in TVET Institutions

Enrollment	2002/2003	2003/2004	2004/2005	2005/2006	2006/2007
Male	17,060	15,889	18,440	16,933	14,622
Female	2,717 (13.7%)	2,783 (14.9%)	2,984 (13.9%)	3,370 (16.6%)	3,383 (18.8%)
Total	19,777	18,672	21,424	20,303	18,005

Source: MOESS 2008

Table 6 Enrollment in TVET Institutions

Special Education

Special education is provided in the country to create educational opportunities for children and youth with special needs at pre-tertiary levels. The purpose is to promote quality equal education, access, and participation by

- developing training programs to update the knowledge and competencies of teachers of the disabled;
- developing programs for early identification and assessment of children with disabilities;
- procuring specialized equipment, gadgets and devices, and materials; and
- cooperating with the universities for the training of teachers and education of people with special needs.

Special education is thus a system that helps to overcome physical-related equity issues. From Table 7, enrollment has been increasing over the period though the female percentage stays below 40 percent. A good way of assessing the enrollment patterns is checking them against statistics on the physically challenged in the country. However, the slow increment over the period and growing number of people with physical challenges who beg on the street shows that there could be more people with disabilities, both males and females, who may need equitable access to education.

Table 7 Enrollment in Special Education Institutions

Enrollment	2001/2002	2002/2003	2003/2004	2004/2005	2005/2006	2006/2007
Male	2,112	2,617	1,509	2,666	2,821	3,004
Female	1,249	1,497	1,694	1,769	1,901	2,088
Total	3,361	4,114	4,203	4,435	4,722	5,092
% Female	37.20%	36.40%	40.30%	39.90%	40.30%	41.00%

Source: MOESS 2008

Table 7 Enrollment in Special Education Institutions

Non-Formal Education

In the provision of non-formal education, a Non-Formal Education Division has been set up to improve the life of illiterate people, especially the rural poor and women, by providing high-quality functional literacy. *According to the definition of a literate person adopted by the UN General Assembly (in 1962) people are considered literate when they have acquired knowledge and skills that enable them to engage in all those activities in which literacy is required for effective functioning in their group and community and whose attainments in reading, writing, and arithmetic make it possible for them to continue to use these skills toward their active participation in the life of their community.* The essence of the non-formal functional literacy program is not to educate adult illiterates to compete with children of formal schools for white-collar jobs, but it is expected that through functional literacy, enrollment levels in basic schools will increase because more people will put their children in school after realizing the benefits of education.

Some results have been realized from the program over the years. It is one program that shows a higher rate of female enrollment than males in all its statistical analysis. Literacy rates showed an increasing trend from 53.4 percent in 2003 to 61.7 percent in 2007. This gives an indication that most of the females who drop out of the formal school system find their way in the functional literacy programs. Much as the program appears to be widening access to education for women (Figure 5), percentage of male enrollment and the female dropout rate will have to be checked for improvement in the National Functional Literacy Program (MOESS 2008).

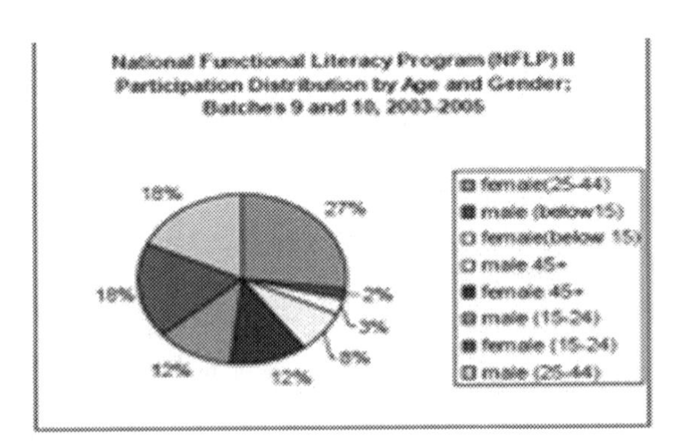

Figure 5 Participation of Males and Females in Non-Formal Literacy Program Source: Agyei-Menah, 2008

Teacher Education

Teacher education prepares the grounds for quality teaching and learning outcomes at the basic education level and develops school-based support for teachers. It has been one of the education avenues for women's empowerment since basic-level teaching has been a key formal employment avenue for female teachers. A comprehensive teacher education program is provided in the country through pre-service and in-service training in order to produce competent, committed, and dedicated teachers to improve the quality of teaching and learning at the basic education level.

As a measure to widen access and improve quality as well, there has been an in-in-out program for all trainees. Under the program trainees spend the first two years of their training in college and are taught using the conventional face-to-face method. In the third year, students spend the year "out" on attachment to schools where they practice teaching and continue their studies using print-based distance learning materials. ICT has also been introduced into the Diploma in Basic Education curriculum.

Other measures for creating equitable access are the district sponsorship of teacher trainees, which has a sponsorship scheme linked to the admission process. The sponsorship scheme aims to address the imbalances in the demand for teachers in rural and other disadvantaged districts. Districts experiencing difficulties in meeting their demand for qualified teachers are allowed to sponsor candidates for training. Such candidates are to be contracted to teach in the districts that sponsor them for a period of at least three years. Out of the total number of trainees admitted over the period the following percentages were sponsored: 2000/2001, 76.7 percent; 2001/2002, 86 percent; 2002/2003, 91.2 percent; 2003/2004, 94.5 percent.

The "access course" for female students is another system for ensuring equity in access. The access course is a special program to increase female enrollment in Teacher-training colleges in order to meet the target of 50:50 ratio by 2015. Female candidates with deficiencies in the minimum requirements for admission are taken through a six-week intensive access course to bring them up to a standard that will qualify them for admission. The first course organized in 2002/2003 enabled 1,500 additional females to be admitted, which brought the total of first-year female enrollment to 3,675. In 2004/2005 the program enabled 1,800 additional females to be admitted, hence increasing the total enrollment of first-year female enrollment to 3,818.

Another measure to meet the Education for All (EFA) goals is the Diploma in Basic Education (DBE) program for untrained teachers. With a total of 24,000 untrained teachers, the Teacher Education Division has been given the mandate to enroll all untrained teachers in a four-year school-based in-service program leading to the award of a Diploma in Education. The first induction course and face-to-face meeting for the untrained teachers program took place in April 2005 in the three northern regions and Afram Plains District.

As a result of the various interventions, the enrollment statistics below indicate some progress in the male-female enrollment ratio over the period. It is anticipated that the access course for female students will help bridge the gender gap in trained teachers for basic education. Having a relatively large percentage of female teachers in the schools will increase the number of female role models and mentors in basic schools, which will obviously help to improve the interest of girls in education right from the basic level. Thus the female teachers will serve as role models and mentors for the girls in all parts of the country.

Table 8Trends of Percentage of Female Teachers Enrolled in Teacher Training Colleges

Enrollment		2003/2004	2004/2005	2005/2006	2006/2007
Intake	Total	8,980	8,989	8,538	9,401
	% Female	43.90%	42%	42.60%	46.60%
Enrollment	Total	23,999	25,116	25,534	26,265
	% Female	40.50%	45%	42.10%	43.05%
Teachers Produced		7,115	7,532	8,300	8,321
No. of Trained Teachers (Public)		86,450	89,669	94,980	52,342

Source: MOESS 2008

Table 8 Trends of Percentage of Female Teachers Enrolled in Teacher-training colleges

Tertiary Education

Tertiary-level education is education offered after the secondary level at a university, polytechnic, specialized institution, open university, and so on to provide training that leads to the award of diploma and degree qualifications (Ghana 2002). In the current knowledge-based economy and the globalization phenomenon, tertiary education plays a vital role in the socioeconomic development of the nation. It has a key role to play in the creation, dissemination, and application of knowledge, in the production of human capital, and in the development of skills and adaptation of knowledge to meet developmental needs. It also has a role to play in strengthening the entire education system and fostering synergies in the entire economy. The existing structure of tertiary education consists of the following:

- A university education of generally four years' duration (longer for professional programs such as medicine and architecture)
- A polytechnic education of three to four years' duration

- A course of study at a professional institute of four years' duration (including a minimum of one-year attachment to schools)
- Specialized institutions offering programs leading to the awarding of degrees and diplomas

Much as a comparison of historical trends with current trends of enrollment in education will give some increase in enrollment, a critical assessment of total enrollments against those who climb the educational ladder up to the tertiary level will indicate that there is limited equitable access to education at that level. On the issue of enrollment in the polytechnics and public universities, there has been some incremental change, but the trend has not changed much The figures in Table 9 and Figure 6 show that the percentage gap between males and females within the 2005/2006 academic year is the narrowest, with 34.7 percent of the total enrollments in public universities being females. In the 1999/2000 academic year, only 26.7 percent of the total enrollment in public universities were females; in the 2000/2001 academic year females made up 29.8 percent of the total enrollment. Females made up 29.2 percent of the enrollment in 2001/2002; 31.5 percent in 2002/2003; 32.5 percent in 2003/2004; 34.5 percent in 2004/2005; 34.7 percent in 2005/2006; 34.3 percent in 2006/2007; and finally, 33.7 percent in 2007/2008.

The issue is more critical at the polytechnics, probably because of the science and technical nature of their courses. For the same period of 1999–2008 the percentage gap between males and females in polytechnics has been narrowing just slightly. Thus the male-female gap is wider. As shown in Figure 7, in the 1999/2000 academic year, only 20.8 percent of the total enrollments in polytechnics were females; in the 2000/2001 academic year, 22.1 percent were females; in 2001/2002, 24.3 percent were females; in 2002/2003, 23.9 percent were females; in 2003/2004, 28.1 percent were females; in 2004/2005, 27.4

percent were females; in 2005/2006, 30.4 percent were females; in 2006/2007, 29.5 percent were females; and in 2007/2008, 29.6 percent were females.

Table 9 Total Student Enrollment for Public Universities and Polytechnics in Ghana

Institution	Gender	Academic Year								
		1999/2000	2000/2001	2001/2002	2002/2003	2003/2004	2004/2005	2005/2006	2006/2007	2007/2008
Public Universities	Male	26,558	28,545	32,693	36,935	43,942	48,055	54,929	58,098	62,267
	Female	9,665 (26.7%)	12,128 (29.8%)	13,491 (29.2%)	16,960 (31.5%)	20,634 (32.5%)	25,353 (34.5%)	29,149 (34.7%)	30,347 (34.3%)	31,706 (33.7%)
	Total	36,223	40,673	46,184	53,895	63,576	73,408	84,078	88,445	93,973
Polytechnics	Male	13,055	14,373	15,456	17,603	17,519	18,138	17,156	20,229	24,241
	Female	3,436 (20.8%)	4,086 (22.1%)	4,976 (24.3%)	5,514 (23.9%)	6,834 (28.1%)	6,845 (27.4%)	7,508 (30.4%)	8,466 (29.4%)	10,207 (29.6%)
	Total	16,491	18,459	20,442	23,117	24,353	24,983	24,664	28,695	34,448

Source: NCTE 2008

Table 9 Total Student Enrollment for Public Universities and Polytechnics in Ghana

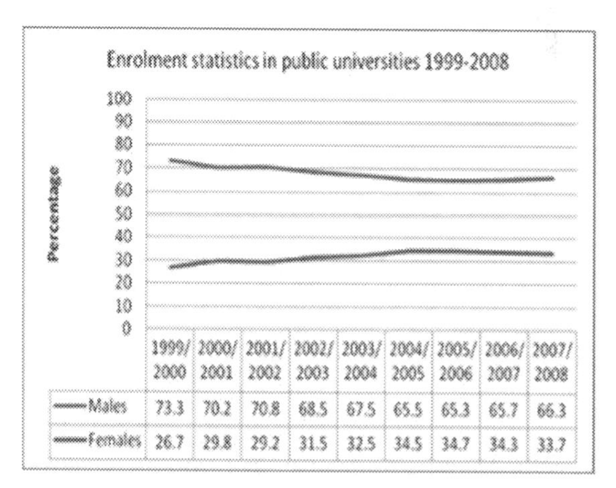

Figure 6 Total Student Enrollment for Public Universities and Polytechnics in Ghana

Source: NCTE 2008

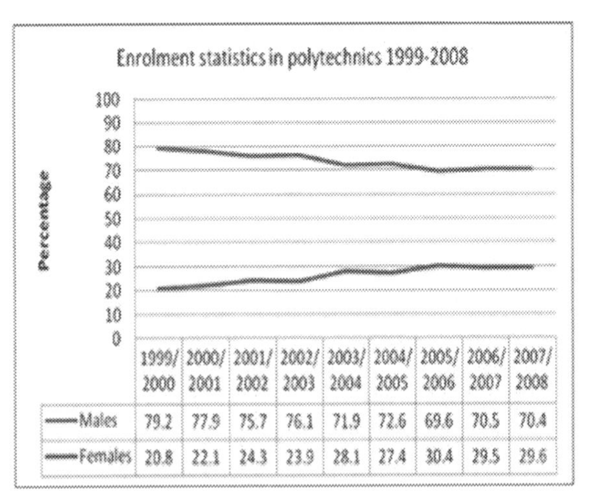

Figure 7 Enrollment Statistics in Polytechnics
Source: NCTE 2008

Emerging Challenges

The analysis of enrollment statistics from the basic to the tertiary level in education revealed some level of increase at all levels and in special programs as well. This is obvious since population has also increased over the period. The critical issue is the achievement of the national norm of a 50:50 ratio at all levels, the targets set in the EFA goals and other educational policies. A more serious issue is the level at which females drop as they climb the educational ladder to the top, or tertiary, level as illustrated in Figure 8. The figure gives a good picture of how narrow the male-female gap in education is at the basic level and how it widens as they climb the educational ladder.

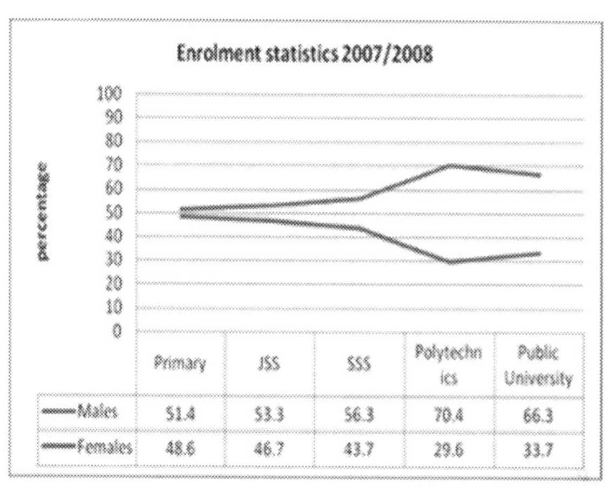

Figure 8 Enrollment Statistics from Basic to Tertiary Level for 2007/2008

In spite of the progress over the years, a critical study of the 2007/2008 academic year as indicated in the graph shows the current state of the gender gap in education from basic (primary) to tertiary (university and polytechnic). The percentage gap between males and females enrolled in polytechnics as plotted on the graph is the widest among the various educational levels. In the 2007/2008 academic year, 48.6 percent of the total enrollments in primary schools were females. In the same period, JHS (JSS) enrolled 571,864 females representing 46.7 percent of the total enrollment. Senior high schools (SHS/SSS) enrolled 191,125 females, representing 43.7 percent of the total enrollment for the same period. Polytechnics also enrolled 10,207 females, representing only 29.6 percent of the total enrollments for the same period. Public universities enrolled a total of 31,706 females, representing 33.7 percent of total enrollments for the 2007/2008 academic year.

This poses a challenge to attainment of equitable access to education. Despite the substantial progress that has been made over the years in providing equitable access to education, the nation continues to grapple with serious challenges in this area.

Much as the inhibiting factors could include poor infrastructure, lack of teacher motivation, and poor supply of learning tools among others, one could highlight the limited access at the tertiary level as a critical issue to deal with. A way out is to fully use open and distance learning, which thrives on information and communication technology to widen access to education at the tertiary level.

Chapter 3

ICT for Education: Policy Initiatives

The country has made the effort to introduce information and communication technologies (ICTs) into the education sector. Initiatives that were undertaken have covered the pre-tertiary through tertiary levels. This is in recognition of the key role ICT can play in widening access to education to a wider section of the population and for facilitating educational delivery and training at all levels as highlighted in the current Education Reforms (2007) and the national ICT policy document of 2004.

The Ghana Information and Communication for Accelerated Development (ICT4AD) Policy

In 2004 Parliament passed into law Ghana's ICT for Accelerated Development (ICT4AD) policy, which is currently at various stages of implementation. This policy represents the vision of Ghana in the information age and addresses fourteen priority focus areas or pillars, among which are the following:

- Accelerating human resource development

- Promoting ICTs in education—the deployment and exploitation of ICTs in education
- Deploying and spreading ICTs in the community

The ICT4AD policy is the result of a three-phase process to develop an ICT-driven socioeconomic development policy and plan that aims to aid Ghana's developmental effort and facilitate the process of becoming a knowledge-based information society and economy in the shortest possible time.

Priority areas of the policy include human resource development, ICT products and services industry development, ICT community buy-in, ICT physical infrastructure development, and research and development. The overall goal of the policy is to construct an ICT-led socioeconomic development process with the potential to transform Ghana into a middle-income, information-rich, knowledge-based, and technology-driven economy and society (Ghana 2006).

Ghana ICT for Education Policy

In view of the need to have a coordinated, focused, and properly managed approach to the adoption and utilization of ICTs and to maximize the use of ICT in education, the education sector decided to draw up a comprehensive policy on ICT. The policy document is multifaceted. It was not drawn in isolation but based on other sector and national priority documents that include the following:

- World Forum on Education Dakar (2000)
- Report of Educational Reforms in Ghana: Meeting Challenges in the 21st Century (2002)
- ICT in Education Policy Framework—highlights key issues and expected benefits of ICTs in education (2002)

- The Ghana ICT for Accelerated Development (ICT4AD) Policy, which recognizes education as a cross-cutting issue within the national framework
- Ghana Education Strategic Plan 2003–2015: Volumes I and II (2003)
- White Paper on the Report of the Education Reform Review Committee (2004)

Generally the policy document seeks to provide a clear purpose and rationale for how ICTs will be effectively integrated into the education sector, including identifying opportunities, issues, challenges, and strategies that will be employed. Again the policy seeks to develop the requisite human resources for the country to meet the demand of the labor market, locally and internationally. The vision of the ICT in Education policy is to use appropriate ICTs to support and align the sector ministry's policies, objectives, and strategies, particularly as it relates to equitable access to education, quality of education, educational management, science and technology, and labor market needs.

The mission of the policy is to articulate the relevance, responsibility, and effectiveness of utilizing ICTs in the education sector, with a view to addressing current sector challenges and equipping Ghanaian learners, students, teachers, and communities in meeting the national and global demands of the twenty-first century.

The fundamental objective of the policy is to ensure that the Ghanaian education sector provides adequate opportunities for Ghanaians to develop the necessary skills, regardless of the levels of education (formal and non-formal) to benefit fully from the information society. In view of this the overall policy goal is to enable graduates from Ghanaian educational institutions—formal and non-formal—to confidently and creatively use ICT tools and resources to develop requisite skills and knowledge needed to be active participants in the global knowledge economy by 2015.

The ICT in Education policy is based on the premise that there are several key elements that underpin the use of ICTs. These include teaching and learning, management and administration, communication, and access to information. Furthermore, it is recognized that these elements will be dependent on policy reforms, within the education sector and other related sectors, including communications, local government, and rural development.

The policy document focuses on seven thematic areas: management, capacity building, infrastructure, ICTs in curriculum, content development, technical support for maintenance, and monitoring.

The policy document acknowledges that if effectively used, ICTs can achieve these things, among others:

- Provide multiple avenues for professional development of both pre-service and in-service teachers, especially through distance education;
- Facilitate improved teaching and learning processes;
- Improve teacher knowledge, skills and attitudes, and even inquiry;
- Improve educational management processes;
- Improve the consistency and quality of instruction both for formal and non-formal education;
- Increase opportunities for more student-centered pedagogical approaches;
- Promote inclusive education by addressing inequalities in gender, language, and disability;
- Widen the traditional sources of information and knowledge;
- Foster collaboration, creativity, and higher-order thinking skills;
- Provide for flexibility of delivery; and

- Reach student populations outside traditional education systems.

On the issue of equity, the policy observes that the use of ICTs in education will have to involve strategic choices about resource allocation. Informed decisions have to be taken about resource allocation with care to avoid cases where technology further amplifies existing in-country digital divides. It is for this reason that the principle of equity will inform the selected approaches and strategies. This must also address the issues of gender and special-needs education.

Concerning access to infrastructure, the expected impact on end-users (learners, teachers, managers, and administrators) will very much depend on affordable and continuous access to hardware, software, and connectivity. This in turn will be dependent on the availability of appropriate physical infrastructure, including classrooms and power sources such as electricity or solar power.

The general policy efforts will be directed at using ICTs to facilitate education and learning within the educational system and promote e-learning and e-education as well as lifelong learning within the population at large. Under the thematic area to use ICT for capacity building, the policy has an objective of using distance education and virtual learning systems to reduce cost and the number of teachers who leave the classroom for study leave. Strategies for achieving the objective include postgraduate distance education for faculty in ICT, building infrastructure to facilitate distance learning for teachers, and setting up digital e-libraries to support open and distance learning programs.

Similarly, in the third thematic area, which is on infrastructure, e-readiness, and equitable access, the policy seeks to facilitate equitable access to ICTs for all schools and communities. Some of the strategies under this theme again seek to develop infrastructure to support distance education and put in systems that will help bridge the rural and urban divides.

The thematic area on content development seeks to develop appropriate content for open, distance, and e-learning. The policy acknowledges the following:

- Digital content is critical to e-education because it can be easily and randomly accessed, adapted and manipulated, and is accessible from many locations.
- Digital content is easier and less expensive to update and distribute.
- Development of digital content will promote the use of indigenous culture in the education system.
- Multimedia digital content can facilitate effective learning.

As part of its strategy under this theme, the policy proposes to

- institute and organize cost-effective distance education programs to cover all levels of education in the formal and informal sectors; and
- promote the development and utilization of a national educational portal/Web site that will provide links to help teachers, students, and the public access educational information readily.

Much as one will question the extent to which some of these strategies have been implemented or will be implemented, it is good to know, at least, that the country has set up these plans. This gives an indication that in response to international trends, the government has the will to use ICT and open and distance learning to provide equitable access to education. A review of the current situation of ICT in the country will tell the extent to which these policy guidelines have been adhered to (Ghana

2007ab; NCTE 2006; Pecku 1998; Reddy and Srivastave 2003; Amoakohene 2005).

Impact of the ICT Policies

With the introduction of the ICT for Accelerated Development (ICT4AD) policy, ICT infrastructural development and services appear to have advanced in the country. Generally, the commitment to improving the quality of education through ICTs is high both at the residential and ministerial levels. Progress has been made on other fronts as well. One of the direct results of the ICT4AD policy is the establishment of the Ghana Information and Communications Technology Directorate (GICTeD) as the operational arm of the Ministry of Communications for ICT policy implementation and coordination of governmental ICT initiatives.

GICTeD is expected to identify and promote the development of innovative technologies, standards, guidelines, and practices among agencies within the national and local governments and the private sector to enable Ghana to become a technology-driven and knowledge- and value-based economy. It is envisaged that GICTeD will help Ghanaians create a world-class online economy and society through its work, as well as developing, overseeing, and coordinating the government's ICT programs on electronic governance and commerce, online services with their associated infrastructure elements, and the Internet (Ghana n.d.).

On the tertiary front, a broadband wireless Internet and voice telephony facility has been inaugurated on the campus of the Kwame Nkrumah University of Science and Technology (KNUST). Known as the KNUST E-Campus Network, the facility has the potential of transforming the mode of teaching and learning on campus, as it would provide members of the university community with in-room and on-campus wireless Internet and voice telephony. The project is the first phase of a comprehensive information communication technology that is aimed at integrating all educational institutions into the global ICT network with KNUST as the hub.

The University of Ghana and KNUST have proposed to run a special regional university under a five-year Pan African tele-education project. With the support of the Indian government and the African Union when completed, the project will provide open access broadband connectivity nationwide at affordable rates. Currently, within the African context, high-speed broadband access, vital to modern businesses, is available in many capital cities and major towns, but it comes at a high price.

The ICT for education policy document has included the provision of ICT computers and the establishment of ICT laboratories, mainly in urban areas. Much as an assessment of reports on the earlier interventions revealed challenges such as lack of policy direction, dependence on external support, and untrained personnel, there have been some achievements as follows:

- A wider number of students and teachers have acquired ICT skills and developed interest in ICT and science.
- The beneficiary schools have been motivated to expand the project and/or acquire more ICT equipment.
- A number of private-public partners, including Parent Teachers Associations (PTAs) and civic groups, have been motivated to support the efforts.

ITU (2009) has noted at the international front that investment in ICT infrastructure in Africa has improved dramatically in recent years, representing a total of US$8 billion in 2005, up from US$3.5 billion in 2000. These figures reflect an increasingly vibrant private sector investment environment, which has been stimulated by the opening of most African telecommunication markets to competition, coupled with the establishment of independent regulators in almost 90 percent of countries in the region.

This increasingly dynamic environment has resulted in lower prices for consumers and significantly widened access to telecommunications, particularly for mobile phone services in urban areas. The African mobile market has been the fastest-growing market of all regions, growing at twice the rate of the global market, with a leap from 16 million to 136 million subscribers between 2000 and 2005. Mobile now outnumbers fixed-line penetration by nearly five to one in Africa. Broadband packages for most of Sub-Saharan Africa show that high-speed access is available, but only at very high prices. On average, broadband prices in Africa are three times higher than in Asia. However, at least ten African countries now offer broadband at below US$15 per 100 Kbits per month.

ITU notes further that one of the striking features of the recent boom in mobile communications is that it is largely African firms—such as MTN, Orascom, or Celtel—that are capitalizing on the new investment opportunities. The boom is as much homegrown as it is based on foreign investment, and it is likely to prove more sustainable than previous rounds of investment in the continent.

Challenges

In spite of the technology breakthrough in Africa, there are in-country challenges that must be noted if Ghana wants to make much progress in the use of ICT for education.

- Access to ICTs still remains highly inadequate and unevenly distributed through Ghana, with an urban bias. There are significant differences in urban and rural access to ICTs.

- The capacity of teachers and educators for ICT usage still remains low. Although some do not have the adequate skills, others are averse to adopting ICTs in the classroom.
- There is inadequate collaboration between the various stakeholders and agencies to check duplication and efficient utilization of resources.
- There is insufficient equipment and slow Internet connectivity because of poor phone lines.

The current world economic crisis could also present some huge challenges. In a news item, ITU (2009) has noted that the financial crisis could have a mixed impact on the global telecommunication/ICT sector. There is evidence that operators are cancelling or postponing their investment plans. If precautions are not taken, the developing part of the world could suffer most.

Another challenge for Africa is not whether or not to integrate into the global economy—that is now a given—but how to become competitive within an integration process that is already taking place. Competitiveness can best be achieved through public/private partnership between firms and government to promote the take-up of new technologies and development of new skills.

There are also challenges with coordination and consolidation of the policy, resources to respond to advocacy issues, the socio-cultural perception about girls and science-related courses, limited access in rural areas, curriculum not being IC concentrated, and issues about sustainability.

Much as there are challenges, the fact remains that ICT for development and education has come to stay. Developing countries have no excuse for not utilizing the full potential of ICT to create equitable access to education. In spite of the challenges, some enabling features have been identified that could support its usage. In the policy documents and implementation efforts there are clear strategies for ICT for education. There is also a policy for gender equity, some level of computer availability and ICT training institutions, commitment of a good proportion of the national budget to education, and adherence to procurement regulations and the political will. The government has also put a priority on human resource development. These indicators could no doubt accelerate an enabling environment for the ICT for the education agenda in the country.

Chapter 4

The State of ICT Service Provision in Ghana

Ghana has been making progress in improving the information and communication technology (ICT) situation in the country. There are policies from the education and telecommunication sectors that outline the government's commitment to the development of ICT infrastructure in the country and also for providing equitable access to education.

It is acknowledged in the country's ICT for development policy that for Ghana to make any appreciable progress in its socioeconomic development efforts, substantial resources have to be directed at improving educational delivery. This is in recognition of the key role ICT can play in widening access to education to a larger section of the population and for facilitating educational delivery and training at all levels as highlighted in the current Education Reforms (2007). Available reports indicate that in the relatively short period since the development of the national ICT vision, Ghana has witnessed appreciable growth in the ICT sector. The Ministry of Communication has reported that the country is likely to exceed the telephone penetration target of the UN's Millennium Development Goal targets for 2015 for telephone lines, cellular subscribers, personal computers in use, and Internet users (Ghana 2008).

In a 2007 World Bank Survey on ICT and Education in Africa, it was remarked in the Ghana country study that compared with other West African countries, Ghana is among the leaders in the use of ICTs. As one of the first African countries to liberalize its telecommunication sector, Ghana has made tremendous progress in ICT infrastructure deployment.

The government of Ghana has placed a strong emphasis on the role of ICT in contributing to the country's economy. The country's medium-term development plan captured in the Ghana Poverty Reduction Strategy Paper (GPRS I&II) and the Education Strategic Plan 2003–2015 all suggest the use of ICT as a means of reaching out to the poor in Ghana. There is also an established ministry dedicated to the provision of ICT infrastructure and services in the country.

The Ministry of Communications

The main machinery responsible for developing infrastructure, services, and other facilities for information technology in Ghana is the Ministry of Communications. The ministry oversees all ICT-related issues. The ministry has a long history dating back to 1958, when it was known as the Ministry of Communications and Works. In the 1970s it was merged with transport to become the Ministry of Transport and Communications until 1997, when a new ministry was created out of the former Ministry of Information and the Communications Division of the erstwhile Ministry of Transport and Communications. This was later changed again to the former name in 2001. These dynamics in the ministry have been in response to local and global developments in communications and the need to capture in full the developmental opportunities and the challenges of the information age. The purpose of the ministry is to enable the government to develop policies that will help integrate communications technologies and public information systems and also harness the full potential of resources for effective communication.

The ministry derives its fundamental existence from Section 13 of Civil Service Law (PNDCL 327) of 1993 as amended by the Civil Service (Amendment) Act, 2001, as follows:

- Initiate and formulate policies, taking into account the needs and aspirations of the people
- Undertake development planning in consultation with the National Development Planning Commission
- Coordinate, monitor, and evaluate the efficiency and effectiveness of the performance of the sector
- Develop the telecommunications, postal, courier, and meteorological services sector
- Provide accessibility to and application of information technologies, as well as development and enhancement of human capability in the use and application of information technologies
- Improve the performance of ICT institutions, especially in broadcasting (technical) and the Internet, especially in encouraging high technical and professional standards and financial/investor support for the sector

The ministry has thus been responsible for all information technology–related activities in the country. Existence of such machinery will no doubt facilitate the implementation of the various ICT policies for education.

Telecommunication and Internet Services

The Ministry for Communications has reported that Ghana is on course to meet and exceed telephone penetration targets for universal Internet access by 2012.

Available records from the Ministry of Communications for the year 2007 indicate that telephone subscription has hit the 8 million mark, giving a telephone density of nearly 40 percent. Fixed lines had increased to 376,509 by the end of 2007, from 248,900 lines in 2001. During the same period the number of mobile phone users rose from 215,000 in 2001 to 7.6 million. Telephone penetration at the end of the period was 36.3 percent. Mobile phone services cover all ten regions in the country, Internet subscription is estimated at 1.5 million users, and broadband subscribers number just over 13,000.

The first phase of the country's fiber-optic development is complete and is expected to facilitate the deployment of ICT applications nationwide and the speedy implementation of the twenty-year ICT4D policy (PCWorld 2008; Aggrey 2008).

Reports from the ICT sector and tertiary institutions indicate that the Ghanaian tertiary education sector is the most advanced in the deployment and use of ICTs in the country. All the country's major universities have their own separate ICT policy, which includes an ICT fee for students. This enables students to have access to twenty-four-hour computer laboratories with broadband Internet connection. However, not all tertiary institutions in the country are equally endowed, and there are instances where the computer facilities are run purely by the private sector, such as cyber cafés on campuses.

In the basic and secondary education sector, a project to set up computer laboratories in all science schools has led to a significant number of computers being installed across the country. Smart boards and projectors are also available in such schools to facilitate teaching and learning. In schools where ICTs exist, a number of teachers use the Internet for research. As a result a computer fee of GH¢3.00 (US$3.20) is allowed to be paid in most secondary schools. There is, however, a great disparity between public and private schools as well as between urban and rural areas in access to ICTs. The school curriculum and course content is not yet available in electronic mode such as CDs, even though it has been a policy issue for many years.

Service Providers

Available data shows that Ghana has six licensed cellular/ mobile operators: Vodafone (formerly GT Onetouch), MTN, Tigo, Kasapa, Zain, and Glo (Globacom). There are two fixed-line operators: Ghana Telecom (Vodafone) and Westel (now Zain). Per 2009 data there are 28 authorized and 7 operational television broadcasting stations, and 140 authorized and 84 operational FM stations. Details for the period 2000 to 2005 are provided in Table 10 below.

Table 10 Telecommunication Providers and Services 2000–2005

Description	Year(s)					Authorized	Operational
	2000	2001	2002	2003	2004	2005	2005
Fixed-Network Operators	3	3	3	3	3	3	3
Mobile Cellular Operators	4	4	4	4	4	5	5
Teledensity	-	-	-	-	-	13%	13%
Internet Service Providers	29	79	-	112	143	-	-
Pagers	7	7	7	10	10	10	10
Public/Corporate Data Providers	9	12	-	-	-	83	23
VSAT Data Network Operators	14	31	-	96	136	162	57
Broadband Operators	-	-	-	4	4	-	-
Marine Licenses	-	-	-	117	117	-	-
TV Stations	3	-	-	-	-	28	7
Pay per View Cable/Satellite	7	-	-	24	28	-	-
FM Radio Stations	49	-	-	127	137	140	84

Source: Ministry of Communication 2005

Table 10 Telecommunication Providers and Services 2000–2005 Source: Ministry of Communication 2005

The mobile telephony operators have made a substantial inroad into the market over the last years with an estimated mobile subscriber base of 8 million by the end of 2009. Mobile telephony now represents 63 percent of the total telecom market. The rest of the market is represented by fixed-line voice products (18 percent), data services such as Internet/ broadband, leased lines and Virtual Private Networks (VPN) (3 percent), and international traffic (16 percent). The estimated market shares of Areeba (MTN) and GT (Vodaphone) for 2005 are indicated in Figure 9.

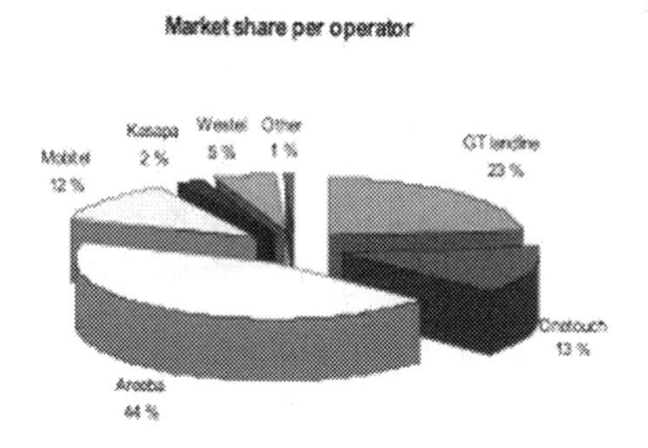

Figure 9 Market Share per Operator Source: National Communication Authority (NCA) data, 2005

Figure 1 shows that MTN has remained the dominant player in the total telecom market with a market share of 44 percent. "GT landline" (23 percent) is voice and data products supplied by the fixed network as well as international traffic. Onetouch (Vodaphone) (13 percent) has passed Tigo (Mobitel) (12 percent) and is now the second mobile operator. Westel's share (5 percent) is represented almost only by international traffic, as their domestic traffic is insignificant. Kasapa (2 percent) is expected to increase its market share with its new mobile technology. The domestic voice market, including mobile, landlines, pay phones, and umbrellacoms, is also dominated by Areeba (MTN 50 percent), followed by GT fixed (17 percent), Onetouch (16 percent), Mobitel (Tigo 14 percent), and Kasapa (3 percent). The distribution of products and services is estimated in Figure 10.

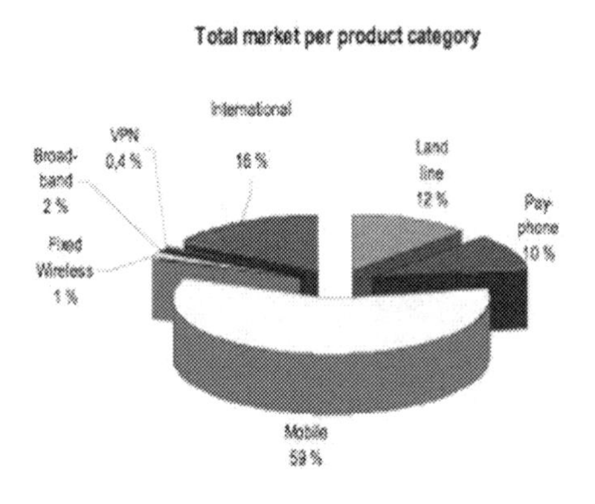

Figure 10 Distribution per Product Category as % of Total Market 2006 Source: National Communication Authority (NCA) data, 2005

Mobile has grown to almost 60 percent of the total market, and international traffic through the licensed operators represents 16 percent. The gray market (international) is not included, neither in the total market estimate nor in the 16 percent share. It should be noted that the landline share of the market has dwindled to 12 percent, only slightly above pay phones of 10 percent. In the pay phone estimate the so-called "umbrellacoms" (Space to Space, One4All etc.) are included. These networks could be used to support distance education activities in the country. The table shows some of the licenses issued for telecommunication services.

Table 11 Licenses for Telecommunication Services in Ghana

Licensed Operator	Type of License	Comments
Ghana Telecom	PSTN license, including an international gateway license	
Vodafone (GTOnetouch)	Mobile license	Right to deploy fixed wireless
MTN (Scancom/Areeba)	Mobile license International gateway license	Right to deploy fixed wireless
Millicom (Mobitel/Buzz/Tigo)	Mobile license International gateway license	Right to deploy fixed wireless
Kasapa	Mobile license	Right to deploy fixed wireless
Westel	PSTN license, including an international gateway license. Can obtain a mobile license against payment of $27.5 million.	The international termination represents the bulk of their business.
Capital Telecom	Regional PSTN license	No operation in accordance with the license provisions
Internet Ghana	ISP license	Operates a broadband service on the GT fixed network
Zipnet (wireless broadband)	No information on license available	No response to request for information from NCA
NCS	ISP license. No information on license on other services	No response to request for information from NCA
Africa Online	ISP license	

Source: NCA 2005

Table 11 Licences for Telecommunication Services in Ghana Source: NCA 2005

Additionally approximately 100 ISP licenses have been issued as well as a substantial number of VSAT licenses. According to advance information from the regulator there are plans to issue wireless licenses for voice telephony. It has been indicated that two licenses per region will be issued, for a total of twenty. Mobility within each region would be allowed (NCA 2005). The specific services of the various service providers are discussed below.

Ghana Telecom (Vodafone)

Ghana Telecom was born out of the Ghana Post & Telecommunications Corporation, which was established in 1974 under the then Ministry of Transport and Communications to provide postal and telecommunication services in Ghana. Since then the institution has gone through several administrative processes for improving its operations. The vision of Ghana Telecom is "To be a regional model, as a viable business entity and caring organization in meeting the telecommunication needs through total customer care." In the light of the vision, its mission is to provide reliable, efficient, and flexible telecommunication services to customers, with emphasis on innovation, technology, and continuous manpower development, and to meet stakeholders' expectations in attaining regional excellence. Among the core values of the company is to deploy technical capacity to facilitate creativity and leadership in ICT in the country. Ghana Telecom serves both the wholesale and retail telecommunication market. Its products and services include the following:

- Voice (fixed, mobile, and pay phones)
- Broadband and data
- Virtual private networks

Vodafone GSM mobile phone service offers network coverage throughout Ghana and continues to expand its services. The excellent telecommunications technology of Vodafone ensures not only wide network coverage, but also quality service.

The mobile network has a switching capacity of more than 4 million subscribers. The expansion of the mobile network had the following targets to be met by the end of 2007:

- All 137 district capitals to be covered by end of 2007
- 93 percent of the population and 60 percent of Ghana to be covered by the end of 2007
- Approximately 85 percent of major roads to be covered by the end of 2006 and 95 percent by the end of 2007

Vodaphone (GT) is the dominant player in the broadband/ data market. Other players are Internet service providers (ISPs) and a couple of broadband providers. In the business market segment several big companies have built and operate their own internal networks, partly with the help of vendors and service providers. The Vodaphone fixed-network capacity will be expanded and tailored to provide data and broadband services as well as products combining voice and data to all district capitals to facilitate ICT expansion in the country. The company estimates that the expected increase in the demand for data and broadband services will be substantial.

The other mobile operators are also trying to enter the data/ broadband market with MTN, Tigo, and Zain laying their own fiber-optic cables across the country. Kasapa's new CDMA-based wireless technology will also deliver bandwidth and quality superior to the GSM networks. Vodaphone will also be better positioned to offer bundled products (voice/data), which are expected to be in demand in the coming years.

Recognizing that telephone and telecommunication infrastructure helps the public make use of advanced information technology applications for distance learning, e-banking, e-business and so on, Vodafone has started deploying GSM pay phones in second-cycle schools on a pilot basis and plans to cover every school in the country, make the network reach every corner of the country, and make telecommunications available in every aspect of life in the country (Vodaphone 2009). Figures 11 and 12 illustrate their current coverage and projection.

Figure 11 Current Connectivity

Figure 12 Projection Source: Vodaphone 2009

Mobile Telecommunication Network (MTN)

MTN has the vision of becoming "the leading telecomunication service provider in emerging markets" with a mission of "building shareholders' value by ensuring maximum customer satisfaction through providing the latest telecommunication services, at the most economical rates while meeting its social responsibilities as a good corporate citizen and providing growth prospects for its employees" (MTN 2008).

MTN, which started as Scancom Ghana, otherwise called Spacefon, has shown itself to be the market leader in the increasingly competitive mobile telecommunications industry in Ghana. MTN has a wide variety of network services as well as segments. These are specially designed for different kinds of people to enhance their mobile experience. It offers subscribers a wide range of options under pay-monthly and pay-as-you-go services.

After one year of re-branding Mobile Telecommunications Network, the organization is focused on consolidating its position as the leader in the market and fulfilling its commitment of bringing world-class telecommunication services to the country. In this regard, MTN has invested substantially in a Network Expansion Initiative meant to enhance speech quality, improve coverage intensity, and extend coverage to new areas.

MTN has integrated mobile telecommunication services into the development of a brand that has become a lifestyle. This fact is clearly demonstrated by its active involvement in various marketing initiatives that are close to the hearts of subscribers. MTN has responded to these needs by introducing a number of exciting products and services, including roaming, tariffs, BlackBerry phones, data services (Internet services on mobile phone, laptop, or PC), and the recent MTN Zone, which gives discounts to prepaid subscribers.

MTN Ghana launched the 3.5G technology in Ghana in January 2009. This introduces a new step in the evolution in mobile technology in Ghana. *3.5G* is the generic term used for the next generation of mobile communications systems that support the effective delivery of a range of data-oriented services.

MTN acknowledges its responsibility toward its stakeholders to sustain long-term mutual value. In this regard, MTN Ghana has established relationships with governments and community groups to enable them work together to achieve profitability.

The technology also provides more efficient systems for the transmission of existing services such as voice, text, and data, supporting far greater speeds than what is available today. The technology plans to provide more efficient systems for the transmission of existing voice, text, and data services and the overall network quality. MTN also plans to offer mobile broadband and video calling that will enable fast data speed and allow users to see and talk to people they call in real time (MTN 2008).

The map below indicates the coverage of MTN in Ghana

Figure 13 MTN Coverage in Ghana Source: MTN (2008)

Millicom Ghana Ltd. (Tigo)

Millicom International Cellular S.A. (MIC) is a leading global operator of cellular telephony services with several investments across the world. Millicom's portfolio of assets currently comprises seventeen cellular operations and licenses in sixteen countries in Asia, Latin America, and Africa, covering a population under license of approximately 392 million people.

Millicom Ghana Limited is a subsidiary of MIC, best known by many in Ghana simply as Mobitel/Buzz and now known as Tigo. For almost a decade and a half since it pioneered mobile telephony in this part of the world, Millicom Ghana Limited has gained recognition for the leadership role it has played with its introduction of innovations in mobile cellular communication that add value to the services offered. With the introduction of cellular phones in 1992, Millicom Ghana Limited—Mobitel breathed new life into the telecommunications industry, changing the face of business in Ghana with the chosen brand name Mobitel.

In 2002 Millicom Ghana introduced its GSM service under the brand name Buzz GSM. Buzz GSM with its trendy lifestyle image offered very exciting services to its numerous clientele. Mobitel, now called Tigo, has, over the years, been able to maintain a fast rate of subscriber and revenue growth and a very high quality of service. Available data show that Tigo has extended coverage in all ten regions of Ghana. Tigo is constantly expanding its coverage by adding new cities and towns to its countrywide network. The network covers about 90 percent of the Accra-Kumasi highway. Tigo's roaming services give convenience of using the network even outside the country (Tigo n.d.).

Zain

Zain is the latest among the mobile telephone service providers in Ghana. It has more than 56 million customers in twenty-two countries across Africa and the Middle East. The company has invested US$420 million in Ghana. By using the latest technology, Zain reports that it has built the first 3.5G network in West Africa. This will ensure the reliability and quality of the network. Recognizing that Ghana needs and deserves a reliable, good-quality mobile service, the company plans to provide a network that has high voice quality, reliable call connection, and call completion. Aside from providing that basic service the 3.5G network allows subscribers to have cutting-edge technology at their fingertips. The network allows them to send video and picture texts and download Internet content at ultrahigh speeds.

To show their commitment to corporate social responsibility the company intends to make an impact in education with their "Build Our Nation" educational assistance program to schools in deprived areas. Again the company is committed to helping Ghana achieve its Millennium Development Goals by providing the technology to build a telecommunications network in the Millennium village in Bonsaaso, in the Amansie West District of the Ashanti region. By this Zain intends to demonstrate how access to telecommunications services could assist in eradication of extreme poverty and improve the quality of life of the underprivileged.

According to Zain they seek to create an environment where technology, customer care, and corporate social responsibility come together to create a wonderful world (Zain 2009).

The activities of the telecommunication operators in the country have shown the extent of coverage and the nature of services and products that are available. The networks and telecommunication services provided by Vodaphone, MTN,

Tigo, and Zain could be used to support distance education activities in the country.

On a general note, the state of ICT service provision in the country shows that ICT infrastructure development and services appear to have advanced. The commitment to improving the quality of education through ICTs is high. Much as there could be challenges with even distribution of ICT infrastructure and limited human resources for fully utilizing the existing facilities and services, there is also a window of opportunity. The various policies and initiatives have contributed to improve the availability of ICT facilities, tools, and services in the country. As a result there has been a modest increment in the use of mobile telephony and access to Internet services. These resources have mostly been used for all sorts of business and official activities, phone calls, text messaging, and e-mailing for personal communication, and other browsing and entertainment activities mostly among youth. If the country has facilities for such activities, then the question for providers of education is how they, especially those who offer distance learning courses, could utilize the available (no matter how little) ICT facilities, tools, services, or resources to improve the delivery of open and distance learning programs in the country. In other words, how do we practically translate the usage of available services for educational purposes, especially ODL?

Part 2 Open and Distance Learning (ODL)

Chapter 5

Open and Distance Learning: An Overview

Open and distance learning (ODL), operating under different terms such as *distance education, distance teaching,* and *distance learning,* has existed for about a hundred years in the more developed regions and for one or two generations in the developing regions. Referring to the Latin American Congress for Open and Distance Higher Education held in August 2001, UNESCO (2002) has indicated that one of the biggest trends of the universities in the last century is the establishment and development of distance education systems. When distance education systems came into existence in the seventies, a frequent criticism was that these were universities from which degrees were awarded by post. In three decades, the concepts have been inverted, naturally aided by the utilization of new computing and telecommunication technologies. The distance education trend has become so strong that it is assumed that by the end of the next decade, *traditional* universities as we know them will have disappeared. For some people what is happening with ODL is an educational revolution, the first major change in higher education in seven centuries (Kramarae 2001).

The traditional notion of education is the type of teaching and learning that occurs in personal contact between the teacher and the learner in the classroom. That is the perception and experience that teaching and learning take place at same time and same place. But gradually with the introduction of new information and communication technology, including printed materials for correspondence, it came to light that formal, informal, or non-formal teaching and learning could also be done via technology. The rapid development in learning theories and advancement in technology has made it possible to shift from institution-led learning to own-time self-learning at a distance. Thus there is a trend from face-to-face teaching to self-paced learning that is gradually moving toward flexibility and openness. It is this experience that has progressed to the alternative delivery system known as the ODL system (Abrioux 2008ab; Asraf, Swatman, and Hanisch 2007; Bruce, Hagens, and Ellis 2007; Denison and Johanson 2007).

Open and distance learning is an educational term and procedure that is evolving every day because of the dynamic system of information and communication technology (ICT) that it thrives on. The definition and application of ODL have been evolving in parallel with the arrival of newer and more intelligent technologies. With the increasing desire for education at all levels and the commitment to attain the Education for All (EFA) goals coupled with the flexibility and dynamism in ODL, the philosophy is constantly emerging as the most convenient way of responding to the growing need of education. As a philosophy of education, ODL presents the possibility of providing equitable access to education irrespective of the state of a nation or prospective students. According to UNESCO, ODL is breaking the barriers of space and time and provides the population with truly equal opportunity and an efficient way to continue education and personal development in line with the massive and effective access to higher education in the current society of knowledge. It also permits a new type of alliance between universities and business, the state, diverse organizations, and so on. ODL permits the diversification of education aimed at special groups; it has great importance for the education of teachers and international cooperation (COL 2007; Dunlop 2004a; Dodds 1996; COL n.d.). In view of these potentials UNESCO has set clear policies that ODL should be given priority as a way for everyone to access permanent education (UNESCO 2002). COL (2008) also notes that the growth of ODL has resulted from many factors, such as decreases in government subsidies of the public institutions of higher education, increases in costs of higher education at both public and private institutions, increases in qualified applicants at the tertiary level, increases in the number of employed women, reductions in secure, long-term jobs, increases in credential requirements for entry into and continuing work in many jobs, rapid changes in information technologies, and increases in attention to lifelong education. ODL is in use in many developed and developing countries, providing varied educational opportunities to meet the varied needs of learners.

What Is Open and Distance Learning?

The term *open and distance learning* is relatively new in the field of education. Much as it has its roots in relatively older fields such as correspondence courses, distance education and teaching, or distance learning, it is a philosophy of education that has been gaining prominence in the world of education for the past fifteen to twenty years. Like most fast-evolving terms, it is difficult to arrive at one definition for ODL. One way to attempt a definition of it is to give a description of it. COL (2000a) has described ODL in the following ways:

- **Teacher and learner are separated** in time or place, or in both time and place.

- **There is institutional accreditation;** that is, learning is accredited or certified by some institution or agency. This type of learning is distinct from learning through your own effort without the official recognition of a learning institution.
- **It uses mixed-media courseware,** including print, radio and television broadcasts, video- and audiocassettes, computer-based learning, and telecommunications. Courseware tends to be tested and validated before use.
- **Two-way communication** allows learners and tutors to interact, as distinguished from the passive receipt of broadcast signals. Communication can be synchronous or asynchronous.
- **There is the possibility of face-to-face meetings for tutorials,** learner-learner interaction, library study, and laboratory or practice sessions.
- **It uses industrialized processes;** that is, in large-scale open and distance learning operations, labor is divided and tasks are assigned to various staff members who work together in course development teams.

Picking the words separately, Mitra (2008:10) has described ODL as follows:

Open means

- removal of barriers to learning,
- flexible learning opportunity, and
- freedom to learn.

Distance means learning that occurs

- away from an institution,
- with a separation between the teacher and learner, and

- with the use of multimedia for educational communication.

Learning means

- a change in behavior after having gone through a situation that causes the change, and
- the acquisition of knowledge, skills, and attitude that causes a change in behavior.

Put together, Mitra explains ODL as a philosophy of constraint-free learning situations, adopting a methodology of organizing learning experiences at a distance using multimedia and information technology as a means.

These descriptions are leading to an explanation of ODL as a system of education whereby the learner and the provider are separated from each other but use a medium for the teaching-learning engagement.

The concept of openness in ODL is crucial to the ODL philosophy. The conventional system of education has rigid requirements such as entrance qualifications, fixed timetables, fixed venues, fixed content, and assessment. These requirements have been very restrictive. These restrictive requirements deprive some people of access to educational programs. Some of the restrictions could be geographical, social and cultural, gender, and physical disabilities. These are some of the barriers in education that the ODL philosophy overcomes by providing flexible learning options (Alghali, Turay, Thompson, and Kandeh 2005; Alghali and Zackmann 2008).

Meanwhile ODL is seen as an educational philosophy because the principle of "openness" is hardly fully implemented. No educational program is fully open, not even those that have the word *open* attached to their names such as "open universities." There is an element of restriction in all open learning programs. But compared with conventional education that is delivered in the face-to-face mode, all open and distance learning programs offer some level of openness.

In summary one will emphasize that ODL means

- learning at a distance but with the flexibility to choose study time, pace, and place;
- an effective and equitable (i.e., fair) means of providing learning opportunities for people in all situations and of all ages;
- a student-centered approach to education that removes all barriers to access while providing a high degree of learner autonomy and in which the majority of communication between teachers and students occurs at a distance; and
- a flexible and open system that has shifted from institution-led learning to own-time self-learning at a distance.

In an attempt to explain ODL, Bates looks at it from the perspective of the various generations of ODL, enhanced by knowledge of the historical processes that the discipline has gone through. The author indicates that ODL has gone through three generations:

First-generation learners study alone, with limited contact from the educational provider.

This model was typically used for correspondence study and is still used to provide learners with resources they can study independently to prepare for examinations offered by an accrediting body, such as a professional organization or a university.

Second-generation distance education provides learning resources in one or more media and consistent communication between the learner and the tutor and, sometimes, additional learning support from the educational provider. This approach is used in many situations in which distance learners study alone, rather than in groups.

Third-generation distance learning provides learning resources in one or more media and interaction among learners as well as between the tutor and learner. Interaction may be via conferencing technologies (audio, video, computer), e-mail, or face-to-face meetings and is used when group learning is combined with individual learning.

Otto Peters has provided the following principles, which are embraced in the ODL system:

- The equality principle—the acquisition of knowledge, skills, and attitudes are open to all; nobody is excluded.
- The principle of equality of opportunity—Traditional barriers to education are removed, including economic difficulties for low-income groups, gender-specific educational practices, unfavorable socio-cultural milieus, or members of minority groups.
- The principle of lifelong and ubiquitous learning—Learning is bound to neither definite life cycles nor definite locations and times. It is possible to learn anytime and anywhere.
- The principle of open curricula—Teaching programs may not be completely developed and determined beforehand in an empirical, scientific manner, but are open and able to respond to unforeseen developments in the buildup of the individual's ability to act.
- The principle of relatedness—The course of learning is not stipulated rigidly and independently of the students, but starts from and is shaped by his or her individual values, perspectives, interests, and experiences.

- The principle of autonomous learning—Learning and teaching institutions are created in which students can organize their learning themselves.
- The principle of learning through communication and interaction—The learning itself is not initiated and steered by means of ritualized presentation and reception processes, but by discussions and active management.
- The principle of relatedness to everyday life—The learning does not take place in relatively enclosed institutions that are defined by bureaucratic structures, but is opened up by keeping to the practices of everyday life (Mitra 2008).

Types of ODL Institutions

ODL has been practiced differently in different countries. This presents us with different versions of the system. There are three main types of ODL institutions, which include single-mode, dual-mode, and consortium.

Single-Mode ODL Institutions

This type of ODL institution solely provides education at a distance. Thus it is set up to offer only programs of study at a distance. They could offer some face-to-face interactions as a supplement to support their distance learners. This could even be optional in most cases. In the single-mode ODL institutions, the teaching and learning process is usually mediated by print, including correspondence; audio, including radio (one-way, two-way), cassettes, telephone or audio conferences; video, including television (one-way, two-way), cassettes, or videoconferences; computer, including computer-based training, e-mail, computer conferencing, or World Wide Web. Most of the world's mega-universities, including Indira

Gandhi National Open University, United Kingdom Open University, and Nigeria Open University, are single-mode ODL institutions.

Dual-Mode ODL Institutions

These are educational institutions that offer two modes. Such institutions use traditional classroom-based methods and distance methods as well. In practice the institution may choose to offer the same programs in both modes using common faculty members, the same entry qualifications, the same application procedures, the same course content, and similar assessments. There could be some inbuilt restrictions such as the inability to cross over registrations. The University of Ghana, the University of Cape Coast, and the Kwame Nkrumah University of Science and Technology are good examples of dual-mode institutions.

Mixed-Mode ODL Institution

Mixed-mode institutions offer learners a wide choice of modes of study that ranges from independent, group-based to some combination with face-to-face. Such institutions maximize flexibility of place and pace of study. The institutions lend even more flexibility to learners by offering a variety of learning opportunities, including face-to-face, distance, individual, or group-based study. The setup could result from convergence of face-to-face and distance modes, and increasingly characterizes organizations that were once single mode or dual mode. Deakin University and Murdoch University, both in Australia, provide examples of institutions that are now mixed mode. An advantage for the mixed mode is the opportunity to draw upon the resources of the resident faculty and services. Meanwhile such systems could have several complexities that will call for well-laid-down regulations and effective organization. Faculty could also be overburdened if staff strength is not increased.

Consortium

A fourth type of ODL institution is a consortium. A consortium is a group of institutions or ODL programs devoted to broadening or sharing ODL programming. Two or more ODL institutions may share resources, which could be in either the designing or delivery of programs, or both. They could also share other resources such as ICT facilities. Institutions that are in the process of building up their own resources and facilities could form a consortium with an established institution to start with. There could be occasional administrative problems in this arrangement if the rules of the game are not well outlined in the beginning. Although the University of Mid-America is seen to have failed in its attempt at a consortium, the Mind Extension University has some success stories to share in this endeavor (Jeffries n.d.).

Application of ODL to Types and Levels of Education

ODL is applicable to all aspects of education, be it at the basic level, secondary level, or tertiary level. Some ODL systems provide courses for school-age children. There have been cases of interactive radio instruction with primary-school children, but most secondary school-age provision is characterized by high dropout rates. Most systems are aimed at adult/post-school populations. ODL has been more successful with post-school programs for adults. ODL has also been extensively used for teachers to upgrade their skills without leaving the classroom, especially in countries with low teacher enrollment. Currently there has been much focus on using ODL to provide basic education for all, adult education for increasing access to higher education, renewing and diversifying education systems, teacher training, higher education as a way to increase access for creating high-quality systems of education, and building the capacity of the adult working population in all aspects they may require (Moore and Tait 2002; COL 2004a). Specific areas of application of ODL are discussed in detail in the section that follows.

Non-Formal Education Programs

There is much potential in ODL for non-formal and community development sectors of education that have not been fully realized. Just as technology began to be used more widely in education, enthusiasm for basic adult education grew in the 1960s and 1970s. Mass communication approaches supported with some face-to-face group discussions have served as a means of delivering a wide range of educational and skills programs in support of agriculture, health and nutrition, governance, commerce, democratic processes, and other areas of development to the adult population. Most of the ODL non-formal programs have focused on adult learners, especially in rural districts. The largest use is reported to have been on short courses to help farmers and small businesses adapt to new technologies, which has remained the most common usage worldwide. Some institutions have also focused on delivery of programs on marital relations, personality development, aging, child care, first aid, vocational skills, and entrepreneurial development, to illiterate adults, new literates, less educated adults, leprosy patients, and unemployed youths, among others.

COL (2003) reports that an early and influential prototype, the Canadian Farm Forums of the 1940s, suggested a way forward through the motto "Read, listen, discuss, act," an approach that was later used in India and Ghana. Radio, for instance, has been a very powerful tool in non-formal education. The radio campaigns were an earlier ODL model used to deliver short, highly intensive campaigns to support major development ends. Some of the early radio projects were designed to break free of the parts of the school syllabus that were irrelevant to adults. Through the adult-focused programs, content was designed to offer a curriculum of more practical use to the adult population. An example is given of Botswana, where the approach was used in 1976 to raise awareness of a new policy for cattle on tribally owned land. Radio and television dramas have also been used in Ghana and countries such as Gambia and Nigeria as a means of educating people about health issues such as family planning and HIV/AIDS. The Institute of Adult Education, Non-formal Education Division, and non-governmental organizations have been very active in promoting non-formal educational programs in Ghana on the airwaves. It is unfortunate that the strong desire by the government to invest in formal educational programs curbed the enthusiasm for non-formal programs.

Secondary-Level Education

ODL has been used systematically to support conventional systems at secondary levels. Spronk (1990) indicates that the most rapidly growing distance learning sector is the pre-university age group. This is an exploding market, and universities are increasingly providing middle-school students with advanced course programs for which there is not enough demand at their local school to allocate the resources, but that can prove profitable when made available to students at all the area secondary schools. In the history of ODL in Ghana it is reported that during the correspondence era in the 1970s, the Institute of Adult Education and some foreign institutions delivered courses to the adult population to prepare them to write the General Certificate Ordinary/Advanced Level Examinations, which could qualify them to gain admission to the universities. Some also used the certificates to earn a living by getting employment to do clerical or what they called "white-collor" jobs.

Tertiary Education

ODL has been very prominent at the higher education level. Over the years developing countries have used it as a means of widening access to education at that higher level. COL (2003) indicates that this has been the practice since the invention of the distance education method near the end of the nineteenth century, when the use of new technology (i.e., national rail systems that supported national postal systems) made it possible to deliver higher education beyond the boundaries of the campus, especially in such new and large nations as the United States, Canada, Australia, South Africa, and Russia. These countries have led the way in the use of radio for university-level teaching, then television, and today the Internet.

The development of the Open University in the United Kingdom introduced some innovativeness in the provision of ODL programs at the tertiary level. The Open University provided the model for the integrated multimedia systems approach to the delivery of higher education by a single-mode university. This model has been emulated in several other countries. Most of the open universities have developed into mega-universities with more than 100,000 students. In Ghana there is a government policy to turn all the public universities into dual-mode universities to offer courses in both the face-to-face and the distance mode. This policy is generating great results. The University of Education, Winneba, which began its ODL program in 1998, has approximately 7,000 students with 53 percent females and 46.5 percent males in its Level 300 for the 2006/2007 school year. University of Cape Coast, which began in 2001, has more than 18,000 students, 49.7 percent females and 50.2 percent males, in the Diploma in Education courses. The University of Ghana, which began its distance education program in 2007 and therefore in its second year of operation, has more than 3,000 students.

Teacher Education

ODL has been used extensively for the training of teachers, pre-service teacher preparation, upgrading of academic qualifications, and in-service continuing professional development in particular subjects, content areas, and instructional methods. There are instances from both developing and developed countries to show that training at a distance could reach large groups of teachers, especially those in remote areas. There have been such initiatives in countries such as Ghana, Burkina Faso, Chile, China, India, Mongolia, Nigeria, and South Africa to prepare new teachers or upgrade the skills of the existing teaching force. In the case of Ghana, ODL has been used to upgrade the certificate of teachers to a diploma status.

ODL for teacher education has been possible in countries with limited ICT infrastructure. In such countries radio, television, and print-based materials, audio- and videocassettes, coupled with optional face-to-face tutorials in local study centers, have been the means of delivering the teacher education programs. The China Television Teacher's College, a part of the China Central Radio and Television University, uses television-based distance education to prepare new teachers and provide a range of distance education professional development programs for primary and secondary teachers, principals, and administrators as well. Brazil's national distance education system, PROFORMAÇÃO, is used to provide initial training to unqualified preschool and primary education teachers and combines self-study and bi-weekly workshops using print-based and video materials. India uses print-based materials to provide a comprehensive child development certification program for teachers. Mongolia uses radio and print-based materials as part of the strategy to help primary teachers transform the teaching-learning process. South Africa is using interactive radio to support teachers of English as a second language. Ghana is using distance education and face-to-face models to supplement those with teacher education certificates obtain diploma and degree certificates. The above examples illustrate some of the ways the available technology resources have been used to provide pre-service and in-service teacher education. Such arrangements could no doubt provide a cost-effective way of widening access to education (UNESCO 2002).

Technical and Vocational Education

Technical and vocational education has been critical for development. It is a specialized area of education that has contributed to the improvement in productivity of a national labor market and helped individuals improve their employment prospects in rapidly changing socioeconomic conditions. This makes open and distance learning very significant in the field of technical and vocational education. ODL has two main functions in contributing to the training of people in technical and vocational fields. First, it responds effectively to the growing demand of working adults or any others who have difficulties getting training in conventional education because of lack of flexibility in the timing and location of courses. Second, it provides an opportunity for the empowerment of those most disadvantaged, such as the unemployed, those with disabilities, women, and ethnic minorities in the existing conventional educational arrangements.

Because of its practical nature, open and distance learning for technical and vocational education has to be supported with intensive experimental work and hands-on training through residential schools, home experiment kits, and videoconferencing arrangements, depending on the available facilities. Electronically supported open and distance learning programs using the World Wide Web are now substantially employed in technical, vocational, and professional education. Many countries have developed vocational, polytechnic, and other types of short-cycle colleges, sometimes spanning both secondary and post-secondary levels. Examples of such institutions include the Australian colleges and the U.S. community colleges.

Benefits of ODL

Continuing education and training is an expanding field that is making good use of open and distance learning. The growing need for recurrent and continuous updating of knowledge and skills is a fundamental demand in today's knowledge-based society. Open and distance learning with its decentralized and flexible delivery and its modular structure of courses and curricula has become an obvious way of meeting this need. It is also cost-effective for organizations that have to send staff to foreign countries for refresher courses.

Open and distance learning institutions are developing particular courses for particular needs in this direction. This is leading to a growth in cooperation and partnerships between enterprises, professional bodies, and distance teaching institutions. Consortia and special training institutions have also been established in some instances to serve particular trades and professions with continuing education courses. Many large corporations provide in-service training at a distance for their employees. The medical profession is another example of a profession that often uses distance education for continuing education purposes. An example of such institutions given by UNESCO (2002) is the National Technological University in the United States, which provides continuing education for engineers through satellite broadcasts from about fifty universities.

One cannot underestimate the tremendous potential that ODL has to offer for human resource development, especially in a developing country. Open and distance learning is not only useful to students. It offers a number of advantages to learners, educational institutions, governments, and employers as well.

For Students

ODL creates lifelong learning or continuing education opportunities for students. Some people drop out of school at an earlier stage in life. As they grow, they gain awareness and develop an interest in pursuing further studies. Some also see the need to enhance themselves to gain promotion in their career. With career and probably family and other communal responsibilities, ODL becomes the only option for such people to respond to their educational needs.

ODL overcomes physical distance as well. ODL helps students deal with problems such as distance and time, which can be barriers to conventional learning. Learners in remote locations who are unable or unwilling to physically attend a campus are able to access an educational program through ODL. Some people do not live near or work within the reach of institutions where they want to study, so they enroll in ODL programs to further their studies. Because learners and teachers are geographically separated in this mode of education, students are reached no matter their location.

ODL addresses some personal hindrances to education. Most people, especially women, find it difficult to leave some personal commitments and go to school. Because ODL gives one the chance to combine work, home keeping, and study, such people find it convenient to pursue their educational ambitions via ODL. There are some adults who because of their age feel shy about joining young students in a face-to-face program. For such people ODL programs turn out to be a better option. The physically challenged also get the opportunity to access educational programs from wherever they are. Using wheelchairs to travel, for instance, could be very challenging. Some also have hearing disabilities. With ODL programs their disabilities do not keep them from pursuing their educational ambitions.

ODL offers enhanced quality. Much as there are arguments over the quality of ODL courses compared with those on campus, one could emphasize that in the face of growing numbers of students in on-campus programs where most hardly get access to their professors or the opportunity to ask questions, ODL offers a better quality. The complex design processes of the instructional materials result in a higher quality of course than would be found in the classroom. As the materials go through a series of rigorous processes of writing, editing, and reviewing by teams of experts and professionals, quality is enhanced in the materials that are finally produced. In dual-mode institutions, on-campus students manage to get hold of ODL instructional materials to enhance their studies.

ODL is relatively cost-effective. Compared with on-campus programs whereby students have to pay for tuition in addition to food and accommodation and in some cases quit their jobs, ODL programs have been found to be less expensive. This depends on how one looks at it, but there is the view that life on campus for the adult learner may be much more expensive than keeping one's job, home, and societal responsibilities while studying. If nothing else, one is able to earn income while studying. According to COL (2000a) whatever other claims can be made for ODL, its cost-effectiveness remains the most common reason for its use.

Educational Institutions and Governments

ODL widens access to higher education. With the use of ODL, institutions that have limited space are able to expand their intake and enroll a lot more applicants. There is increasing demand for education, especially at the tertiary level. Most universities have limited space, infrastructure, and other educational facilities to respond to the growing applications. As a university without walls, ODL presents an opportunity to such institutions to increase their enrollment. The system is also able to accommodate low and dispersed enrollment. This is because ODL has no restrictions whatsoever, especially in space. It has the capacity to embrace people of diverse backgrounds.

ODL solves time or scheduling problems. In the face of complex programs, limited lecture halls, and increasing numbers of students, some institutions find it challenging to draw suitable timetables for their students and faculty members. ODL could be used to solve time or scheduling problems for students who find it impossible to attend face-to-face lectures.

ODL complements on-campus studies. The potential of ODL to increase innovation and creativity in conventional education has been experienced in some dual-mode institutions. Some faculty members and students of some dual-mode institutions have found it useful to use the ODL instructional materials to supplement their study materials. The prepared notes are user-friendly and self-instructional, making studies more convenient for students especially students in areas where reading materials such as textbooks are limited. In such dual-mode institutions the introduction of a distance program at a conventional university has led to curriculum reform and new learning materials for resident students in the same subjects (UNESCO 2002; COL 2000b; COL 2002; COL n.d.).

ODL can make the best use of the few teachers available when there is a lack of trained teaching personnel relative to demand. Teachers can be geographically concentrated, or in some instances teachers with certain expertise are in short supply. With ODL the few teachers can be used to reach large numbers of students.

ODL deals with cultural, religious, and political considerations. It can deal with differences, and consequently widen women's opportunities to learn. It also meets the needs of populations affected by violence, war, or displacement. Again ODL makes learning possible even when group assemblies are proscribed. Thus it can embrace people of diverse backgrounds.

Employers

ODL is beneficial to both public and private employers. As part of conditions of services, some workers become entitled to study leave with pay after serving for a number of years. Training and retraining is also very useful in improving work productivity and efficiency. With ODL programs employers could achieve much with little. Thus employees could get the opportunity to combine work and study, which may not require many resources or much commitment from the employer.

Weaknesses and Challenges of ODL Programs

Like every system and practice, it is obvious that ODL will have some drawbacks that will have to be checked for improvement. Just like the benefits, the challenges are applicable to students, the institutions that provide ODL, governments, and employees.

Students

Could be expensive—Much as it has been argued that ODL programs could be relatively cheaper, the type of technology used and the cost of other supporting services and facilities could give the learner an unmanageable financial burden. A solution is for ODL-providing institutions to offer affordable multiple support systems for students so that they can pick and choose according to their financial ability.

Limited access to ICT facilities and other support systems—Especially in the developing countries where there is limited advancement in ICT infrastructure, most learners are disadvantaged in terms of access to ICT facilities, so if an

ODL programs relies on ICT tools for delivery, a majority of the target population will be left out. Some people could live in areas that are so remote that regular travels to study centers could be a hindrance. Some may also find it difficult to leave their work to attend regular tutorials. That is why it is necessary to use multiple support systems so that students will have the opportunity to pick and choose as it suits their location, career, or entire lifestyle.

Limited programs—Much as almost all kinds of educational programs could be offered at a distance, most ODL institutions restrict the number of programs they offer. Prospective students whose programs of interest are not offered may not be able to enroll. Others may have to choose courses that they may not be very much interested in. Meanwhile an institution's ability to offer one's program of choice is a strong motivating factor for learners. Offering a relatively wide range of courses could be the way to go, but it goes with huge financial investment on the part of the providing institution.

The isolation factor—Unlike the conventional method of education, education at a distance can be very lonely. This was especially true of correspondence programs. If a conscious effort is not made to create interactive platforms, students will remain isolated from each other and their tutors until graduation. Interestingly, a wide range of ICTs have been used to overcome this challenge. Depending on available resources, most ODL institutions have used different communication tools to keep students close to each other as much as possible. In places where there is limited access to or lack of ICT infrastructure, ODL institutions have supported their programs with regular face-to-face interactions. Some institutions have also encouraged distance learners to form small study groups with learners within their communities. In cases where there are no nearby learners, students have been advised to encourage people from their localities to enroll in the program so that they can form study groups (COL 2004a; COL 2004b).

The second-rate factor—There is a misconception among some people, especially those whose experience is limited to that of the conventional method, that certificates obtained from ODL programs are not of a high value standard. It goes to the extent that some employers will hardly recruit someone who has obtained a certificate at a distance. Experience is the best teacher in this case. The only solution is for those who have obtained their degrees at a distance to prove themselves at their workplaces and in society. Some faculty members of dual-mode institutions who have had the opportunity to handle both on-campus and ODL students have testified that in some instances, the ODL students perform better than their peers on campus (Jeffries n.d.).

Providing Institutions and Government

Some institutions and governments have found it very difficult to kick-start ODL programs to solve the problems of increasing numbers of applicants. Several factors have contributed to this.

Huge initial investment—Much as ODL programs have been found to be relatively cheaper compared with on-campus programs, many resources are required at the initial stages. Development of course materials alone can be capital intensive. Support services and running costs also require financial investments. Developing countries have other pressing demands and therefore in most cases have found it difficult to invest much in ODL programs. Development organizations have supported some developing countries at the initial stages, for instance, by training instructional designers and providing some start-up capital. What most governments and institutions have successfully done on their own to overcome this hurdle is to charge relatively cost-effective fees that can be used to manage the program. This strategy has worked very well for the institutions and governments that have been able to make such bold decisions.

Excessive demands from faculty—In order to ensure parity of standard in both on-campus and ODL programs, some dual-mode institutions have made it a policy to use the faculty members who teach on-campus students to develop the instructional materials, administer examinations, and assess students. This has put a lot of stress on already overburdened faculty. Such institutions may have to start thinking about recruiting more faculty members to support the existing ones. This has financial implications, though. Maybe some of the resources from the students' fees could be used to remunerate the extra recruitments.

Employers

Abuse of the system—The awareness of and desire to pursue further studies is very high among employees. With ODL providing the opportunity to work and study, most employers take undue advantage of the system. The combination of the two roles affects some people's commitment to work. In institutions where monitoring and supervision is not done effectively, lateness to work and absenteeism increases among some of the members of the staff who enroll in ODL programs. Employers and employees will have to strike a deal in such a way that job performance and human resource development will not suffer in the process.

ODL has emerged as a sure way of responding to the growing educational needs of the present century. With continuous technological advancement and the rising need for continuing education, ODL has been seen as a system of education that fits the busy lifestyle of the working adult population. Most working adults don't have any choice but to pursue further studies to keep their jobs or progress in them. Interestingly the ODL mode is also becoming attractive to young adults who have completed their secondary education but could not obtain a very high score to gain admission into on-campus programs in view of the limited space. Governments

Chapter 6

Features of ODL

ODL has a unique way of operating. By its nature of being offered at a distance, extra caution is taken in all aspects of its implementation. Again, since it remains a new area for most people, they find it difficult to comprehend, for instance, the nature and processes of developing the instructional material, how students could be sustained in the program, methods of assessing students, the cost involved, credibility of the certificates, and many other issues. To create a little bit of awareness about the practices of ODL, this chapter covers some of the essential components of implementing an ODL program.

The Instructional Design

Instructional design is the systematic development of instructional specifications using learning and instructional theory to ensure the quality of instruction. It is the entire process of analyzing learning needs and goals and the development of a delivery system to meet those needs. It includes development of instructional materials and activities and tryout ODL situations. Adults learn differently from children. As a result they are taught differently. The teaching-learning engagement must be more specialized, especially when they take their courses at a distance. In ODL the instructional material represents the teacher, and it must be designed as such. The module must embody all that a teacher will do in a face-to-face mode (Wang and Liu n.d.; Williams 2000; World Bank 2009).

In the scope of Malcom Knowles' principles of adult learning, COL (2003) has identified the following characteristics of an adult learner that should inform the design of an instructional material for distance learning:

1. Adults need to know why they are learning.

2. Adults see themselves as responsible, self-directed people.

3. Adults come to post-school education with a wealth of experience.

4. Adults are likely to choose to learn when they are ready to learn.

5. Adults, in their learning, are problem-centered.

6. Adults tend to be motivated by personal factors.

Considering these characteristics of an adult learner, the instructional material should do the following:

- Include opportunities for learners to recall their prior knowledge and experience, and encourage them to reflect on their experience and compare it with what they are learning.
- Design adult curriculum around the needs of learners. *Needs* here refers to why they are learning, such as to qualify for some other course, to start their own business, or to gain a particular type of job. It helps to look at every item in a proposed curriculum and ask, "How will this item be useful to our learners?"

- Look for ways of allowing learners to make choices and direct their own learning by setting some of their own goals or by giving them a choice of tasks.
- Encourage learners to set their own personal goals and to check their progress against them.
- Look for ways in which learners can choose how they complete tasks. For instance, in designing a marketing program, learners might have the choice of preparing a brochure, a poster, or a radio advertisement.
- Try to give learners the maximum opportunity to put new knowledge and skills into practice.

In classroom-based teaching, the basic resource is the teacher. He or she may use other resources such as textbooks or audio-visual aids, but the teacher remains the central component of the system. He or she performs many functions. He or she

- defines what is to be learned;
- provides information;
- explains;
- gives examples;
- asks questions;
- answers learners' questions;
- sets learning tasks, both for individuals and groups;
- grades work;
- checks what learners have learned;
- provides feedback to individual learners on their progress;
- provides other resources such as textbooks;
- gives advice on how to use those resources;
- gives study advice; and
- helps with individual problems through counseling.

In distance learning, there is no teacher. The teacher is replaced by a combination of learning materials and tutors.

Because tutors are expensive and distance learners mostly study at home, the tutors are involved with learners only for short periods. This means that the learning materials have to carry out all the tasks of the classroom teacher, except for grading work. In other words, the learning materials themselves will define what is to be learned, provide information, give examples, and carry out all other teaching tasks.

Creating materials that can do this is a complex technical task. This makes instructional design very critical. There is no prescriptive list of the tasks that an instructional designer carries out in turning theory into day-to-day work, but the following are typical:

- Determine what the learners need to know (a stage often called *learning needs analysis* or *training needs analysis*).
- Develop learning outcomes.
- Decide how learning will be assessed at the end of the course (or during the course if the assessment is in stages).
- Allocate outcomes to the various sections of the course (usually called units).
- For each unit:
  - decide the types of activity needed to achieve each outcome;
  - decide the examples needed to help learners learn each outcome,
  - identify any graphics needed, and
  - plan any self-assessment needed for that unit.
- Write the units.
- Test and evaluate the materials.
- Revise to take account of the evaluation results (COL 2003).

After the materials have been developed through the processes that have been described above, they are then delivered using either print or electronic media. Examples of electronic media include the Internet (e-learning or online), compact discs, videoconferencing, television, or radio broadcast. A mixed-approach delivery could be used, depending on the location of students, the resources or facilities available, timely delivery, and the urgency of material to be delivered.

Students' Support Systems

Learners who take open and distance education courses are given special support for several reasons. Distance learners are faced with study and learning difficulties, problems of interacting at a distance, managing their time, overcoming isolation, and other personal problems that call for some form of support to motivate them to stay in the program.

There could be a high level of dropout or failure if the students are not supported. Student support has universally been seen as a range of services offered to students that they can choose to use or ignore. However, this view has been challenged on the grounds that students who most need these services are the ones least likely to use them (Roberts n.d.). This is probably because not all students have the capability and resources to access the support services. This implies that conscious effort has to be made to offer all support services accessible to all students no matter the location, income level, gender, color, tribe, or race (Tait 2003; Tait and Mills 2002; Tait 2000).

There is also the perception that all distance learners need is well-developed instructional materials. Once students have that, there is no need to provide additional support. This thinking appears to belong to the era of correspondence education, but it is not true in this generation, where there has been so much advancement in information technology. Keegan's (1990) definition of students support in Roberts (n.d.) refutes this idea. For Keegan, student support is "the planning and preparation of learning materials and the provision of student support that distinguishes distance education from private study and teach yourself programs—correspondence education." The support system is vital to the success of an ODL program. It serves as the interface between the institution and its students.

In an attempt to define learner support, Roberts (n.d.) outlines a wide range of definitions that help to bring out the meaning of the concept:

- The requisite student service essential to ensure the successful delivery of learning experiences at a distance (Wright 1991)
- The elements of an open learning system capable of responding to a particular individual learning (Thorpe 2002)
- The support incorporated within the self-learning materials, the learning system, and assignment grading focusing very specifically on the courseware, the exercise of learning, and assessment (Hui 1989)

All these definitions highlight the fact that the support is designed to assist students in the ODL programs. Such support could vary to include regular personal contact between learners and support agents, contact among learners, supplementary study materials, and access to several resources and facilities, among others.

Students who study at a distance are faced with enormous challenges. Some of the challenges that ODL students face include the following:

- Difficulty in understanding course content
- Unhelpful course information
- Dissatisfaction with tutorials

- Feeling lonely and isolated
- Not sure where to get help
- A feeling of being left in the dark
- Not able to manage time properly between work, family, and study responsibilities
- No study plan
- No convenient place to study
- Inability to attend tutorials or visit study centers
- Financial crisis
- Other personal and health problems

Details have been provided in Table 12.

Table 12 Typical Student Problems

Type of difficulty	Examples
Study and learning	• Managing their time • Preparing written works such as assignments and essays • Being able to learn from text (students often see text as something to be learnt by heart and lack strategies for understanding and critiquing text) • Understanding difficult material • Dissatisfaction with tutorials
Interacting at a distance	• Feeling isolated and alone • Feeling that he/she is different from the other students, e.g. they are cleverer, they understand the course better than I do • Not knowing who to contact about various problems • Being in awe of tutors and staff whom they have never met • Not having the skills to initiate and sustain relationships at a distance
Personal	• Lack of a place to study • Lack of access to libraries • Not able to attend tutorials or local centre activities • Family or work commitments • Financial costs

Source: COL 2004a

Table 12 Typical Student Problems Source: COL 2004a

In view of these and many other problems, students will have to be supported by any of these possible means:

- Break down the students' isolation through tutorials, telephone/online conferences, newsletters, or radio programs.
- Respond to particular problems by tutors' advice on time management or planning assignments
- Build up the students' study skills and self-confidence by teaching them study skills or through encouraging reflective learning
- Help students manage their time and study effectively by preparing written work such as assignments and essays, assisting them to learn from text or understand difficult material
- Give timely feedback (COL 2003).

Support could vary from community to community and or person to person. An institution will have to analyze the peculiar problems of the students and design support systems to respond appropriately. Some of the general support measures for students have included

- orientation programs,
- regular or constant correspondence with tutors via letter or e-mail,
- telephone discussion with tutors,
- telephone/online discussions led by tutors,
- videoconferences,
- tutorials,
- weekend study sessions,
- field trips,
- newsletters and newspapers,
- radio tutorials,
- self-help groups,
- social events,
- course Web sites,
- group discussions,

- regular face-to-face interactions,
- formative assessment measures, and
- online interactive programs.

The Tutor Role in ODL

In view of the peculiar nature of ODL, tutoring forms an essential component of the system. Like the support systems that students require to be successful in ODL programs, the role of the tutor is central to the success of an ODL program. Tutors are just one means of supporting learners, but they are widely seen as the most important component of a support system. "Tutors are the most crucial form of learner support. Without tutorial support, the best materials in the world may prove disappointing" (Rowntree 1997, 115, in COL 2004b). As such, tutoring is given special attention in the implementation of every ODL program. In ODL the tutor is the person who mediates between the institution and the student in the entire teaching-learning process. This responsibility goes with several academic activities. The tutor is expected to serve as an academic adviser for students on choice of courses, options for continuing or completing a study program, career choices, clarifying course materials when necessary, developing additional resources or tutorial materials, helping learners develop specific skills, facilitation, information about additional resources for learners who want to pursue a particular interest in greater depth, assessment procedures, feedback on assignments, planning group discussions, and any other educational or administrative activity that will support the students.

The role of the tutor is unique from that of the face-to-face teacher. The differences center on the fact that ODL courses are based on prepared learning materials, so the tutors have no need to prepare lessons as they would in face-to-face teaching. In ODL the tutor is not expected to reteach the content of the materials but rather to help learners make their own sense of what they are learning (McPherson and Nunes 2004).

Meanwhile there are instances where students attend tutorials with the expectation of being taught by the tutor. This expectation, though, confuses the role of the tutor and puts most tutors in a dilemma. If it is not carefully handled, the tutor may end up being unprofessional and his or her sessions may not be participatory as expected in a tutorial class. Considering the essential role of the tutor in ODL, COL (2003) has identified the attributes of an ideal tutor as follows:

- Provides clear explanations about his or her expectations and grading style
- Welcomes extra questions
- Locates one's faults but kindly corrects them
- Makes thorough but cheerful and constructive comments
- Gives an extra boost to encourage a student in difficulties
- Clarifies points that have not been easily grasped or correctly learned
- Helpful in achieving the student's objectives
- Offers flexibility when it is needed
- Shows a genuine interest in motivating learners (even those who are beginners and are therefore at a perhaps less interesting stage for the tutor)
- Writes all corrections legibly and at a meaningful level of detail
- Returns assignments promptly

With these attributes, such a tutor is expected to be consistent, fair, professional in standards and attitudes, encouraging but honest, unbiased, kind, positive, respectful and accepting of students' ideas, patient, personal, tolerant, appreciative, understanding, and helpful in every ODL program.

These kinds of responsibilities require some sort of skills and orientation. In view of this, tutors are mostly trained to be able to do the job in a professional manner. The tutor will therefore have to be trained to have facilitation skills, effective communication skills, and counseling skills, be well informed about the content of the courses to be tutored, and have any other skills and knowledge that will be useful for the job.

Assessment in ODL

The question for most people is how distance learners are assessed. They can't imagine how students who do not attend regular classes can be assessed. And for some, even if they can think of a possible means of assessment, they might not be sure how effective this kind of assessment could be. But the answer is very simple. If on-campus students can be assessed, then distance learners can also be assessed. The procedure may or may not vary. Again if it is possible to teach students at a distance, then they can be assessed at a distance as well.

It is true, however, that although the assessment options are similar to those used in face-to-face education, there are some practical difficulties in assessing students at a distance. There is an observation that distance education has long had trouble with testing. The delivery of testing materials is fairly straightforward, which makes sure it is available to the student and he or she can read it at their leisure, but the problem arises when the student has to do assignments or write tests. The question is this: how do you monitor? If on-campus students can cheat on assignments, tests, and even examinations, how do you check this in a situation where the student and the teacher are separated in both time and space? Although in a classroom situation a teacher could monitor students and visually uphold a level of integrity consistent with an institution's reputation, it could be very challenging to ensure this at a distance. In view of this, those teaching online courses have had difficulty with controlling cheating on quizzes, tests, or examinations, which is still a challenge to most on-campus institutions as well.

But there has always been a way out. For instance some schools address integrity issues concerning testing by requiring students to take examinations in a controlled setting. There has been a strategy for ensuring integrity in assignments as well. Assignments in ODL have been adapted by becoming peculiar to a person's situation, larger, longer, or more thorough so as to test for knowledge by forcing the student to research the subject and prove they have done the work. Quizzes are a popular form of testing knowledge, and many courses go by the honor system regarding cheating. Even if the student is checking questions in the textbook or online, there may be an enforced time limit or the quiz may be worth so little in the overall grade that it becomes inconsequential. Mid-term and final examinations and other bigger tests have in some cases been controlled by assembling students at a central point under supervision. In some dual-mode institutions distance learners are obliged to take the exams at the university or a common location and go through the same process as their peers on-campus. As a standardization measure the examination questions are set and supervised by professors of the university.

This sort of arrangement could limit the flexibility in the ODL philosophy, but students will have to comply for accreditation purposes and also to give high credibility to their degrees. As a result ODL has faced criticism for using assessment methods that are seen as incompatible with an open, student-centered approach to education. In every ODL system there are built-in checks and balances. Examinations are thus necessary in an ODL system for the reasons that the learner may be less known to the tutors and proof will be needed to be sure that the work submitted by the student is really theirs. Besides, based on the expectations and standards of some institutions, probably only examinations could give the system credibility, accreditation, and even respectability in the public eye.

Several measures have been adopted by various institutions to make their assessment procedures credible. In some institutions, in combination with proctors a prearranged supervisor trusted with overseeing big tests and examinations may be used to increase security. With the advancement in technology, secure examination software and packages have been developed to help professors manage their students more effectively. There is no doubt that because of its automatic setups, some of these electronic packages could be more secure than manual methods especially in terms of control of time and other checks for authenticity and credibility.

It will be helpful to explore some of the specific methods of assessing distance learners. Similar to on-campus programs, assessments in ODL can be formative or summative. Formative assessment comprises all the activities designed to motivate, enhance understanding, and provide learners with an indication of their progress. This kind of assessment goes on throughout the period of study, be it by term or by semester. In the classroom situation, formative assessment is given informally as the teacher responds to individual questions or discusses individual pieces of work. Examples of organized formative assessments include short tests, quizzes, assignments, and the activities that are built into the instructional materials. Formative assessments are very useful for distance learners in several ways. It is as important for their effective studies as the tutor support. One could even perceive it as a form of supportive mechanism because it keeps students on their toes throughout the period of study. Timely feedback from the formative assessments becomes critical then. In the ODL system some of the devices that are used to give formative feedback include the following:

- Activities in course materials
- Self-assessment or progress tests in course materials
- Comments of tutors on assignments and other assessed write-ups

- Tutors' responses to specific student questions, be it over the phone or by e-mail
- Comments during tutorials whether face-to-face, by phone, or online
- Comments from peers during study group discussions or in other informal interactions (COL 2003)

It is more useful and effective when it is counted as part of the credits for their continuous assessment. However, if it is counted as part of the overall credits, then much precaution has to be taken to ensure its credibility; otherwise it could be abused.

For a formative assessment to be effective, COL (2003) recommends that the feedback should

- be prompt or immediate, frequent or regular, and continuous;
- seek to help students to avoid making errors, rather than correcting them;
- prompt students to the right answer rather than telling them the right answer;
- always inform students why their answers were right or wrong;
- offer complete explanations as to why an answer was right or wrong; and
- tell the student the direction of their error rather than simply stating that their answer is wrong.

These precautions if adhered to will be helpful in making such assessments constructive instead of being destructive and for that matter motivate students to keep going. Thus it will indeed respond to the principle of continuous assessments being "formative."

Summative assessment, on the other hand, is used mostly once in a term or a semester to do an overall examination of the student's performance over the period. An example of the summative assessment is end-of-semester or end-of-term examinations. This could be final examinations, term papers, projects, theses, or portfolio assessments.

ODL students have been assessed in any of the following ways:

- Case studies with tasks or questions
- Completing a graphic outline
- Fill-in-the-blank
- Guided reading with tasks or questions
- Interpreting graphs and diagrams
- Labeling diagrams
- Matching the correct answer
- Multiple choice
- Questions about a text passage
- Select items from a list
- Short-answer questions
- Tables for completion by the learner

Table 13 provides a framework of types of examinations and expectations.

Table 13 Types of Exams

Exam type	Indicative characteristics	Puts a premium on
Closed	• Fixed time period • No use of notes or textbooks • Choice of questions	• Working at speed • Knowledge • Exam technique
Open book	• Fixed time period • Can use own notes and text books • Choice of questions	• Retrieval skills • Synthesis skills
Take-away topic	• Topic set in advance to allow for preparation • Fixed time period when the exam is taken	• Retrieval skills • Selecting information
Take-away question	• Question set in advance to allow for preparation • Fixed time period when the exam is taken	• Retrieval skills • Selecting information

Source: COL 2004a

Table 13 Types of Exams Source: COL 2004a

ODL students can be assessed just like their peers on campus. They can be assessed by tutor-graded assignments, by portfolio, and online as well. In the tutor-marked assignments, the process and nature of feedback is highly essential. In assessing the students' work, the tutor has to teach using his or her comments rather than just grade the paper or make any degrading comments. In the comments the tutor has to engage the student in dialogue such that the student can seek clarification in the process. In the process of engagement the tutor has to encourage the student to reflect on his or her performance rather than just accept the tutor's judgment. Through this evaluative or assessment process, there is a kind of dialogue in the feedback that facilitates comprehension for the distance learner.

Assessment by portfolio is highly compatible with the idea of students taking responsibility for their own learning. Creativity and peculiarity can also be found in a portfolio for assessment. It gives the students a lot of control over the assessment process and enhances his or her capability as an independent learner. In students' portfolios one can find a wide range of their work, assess process and content, collect evidence of student learning throughout the duration of their course, and compile materials to be used beyond assessment such as upgrading a model or project in the future. This could be very bulky though.

The level of advancement in technology is facilitating the use of online assessment. With Internet connection, students are able to submit their assignments and other projects online, take tests, and in some cases obtain instant feedback or results.

Varying assessment methods can be applied to distance learners just as they can be applied to their peers on campus. However, the way will naturally depend on the level of the students, the objectives of the assessment, and resources available to the students. An institution will therefore have to study its students before settling on the assessment procedure. In all the processes, one will have to ensure quality but not make the mistake of compromising on standards, since that is one sure way of removing the inferiority tag on ODL.

Quality Assurance in ODL

Quality has received much attention not only in on-campus programs but ODL systems as well. Assuring the quality of education provision is a fundamental aspect of gaining and maintaining credibility for programs, institutions, and national systems of higher education worldwide. Quality assurance is required in ODL to prove that the quality of student learning is up to the required standard. Quality assurance is a system designed to *prove* and *improve* the quality of an institution's methods, educational products, and outcomes. It is a process that is mainstreamed in all the processes of an ODL program. An institution cannot assure quality in just the instructional design and end there or just in assessment. Quality assurance in ODL is mainstreamed in all the various academic processes such as designing the program, developing and producing learning materials, course delivery, support services, and assessment procedures. A break in the chain in the process of quality assurance will make the system questionable.

Until recently, the terms *quality* and *standards in education* were not defined explicitly.

It was possible to recognize quality without having to define it. However, traditionally, a few criteria have been used to designate institutions and/or their operations as either standard or substandard. First, the traditional benchmarks for a high-quality institution of higher education were adequate infrastructure and well-qualified and experienced faculty.

Second, an institution was required to prescribe and ensure commonly recognized entrance standards and duration of studies for its various courses and programs. Third, an institution needed to prescribe curricular content and an evaluation scheme for each course/program. Last, it required a prescribed scheme for the educational transaction (such as *x* number of lectures, *y* number of tutorials, *z* number of practitioners, and so on) to complete a course/program successfully. All this ensured that the institution was imparting education of a good standard. This has been and generally continues to be the convention in face-to-face education. Similar arrangements apply in ODL programs.

ODL institutions and students stand to gain most from quality assurance measures. A well-set-up and implemented systematic and consistent quality assurance system helps to establish a good reputation and image for an ODL institution. Such a system sets out defined standards of achievement, documents procedures for all identified processes, establishes ways of responding to issues, and outlines clear accountability for outcomes. The result obtained in this process is greater public confidence, more satisfied students who graduate with enviable degrees or grades, and efficient processes and staff who are confident in their jobs. Students are more likely to experience better-quality instruction and have better learning materials and interactions with the institution and its staff, leading to enhanced learning outcomes. Students who benefit from such a system are likely to recommend the institution to colleagues and to take more courses from such institutions.

In specific terms quality can be assured by adopting the following approaches:

- Self-study or self-evaluation
- Peer review by an expert panel
- Use of relevant statistical information and performance indicators, such as completion rates, overall grades, and profitability
- Surveys of key stakeholders such as students, graduates, and employers

Others include

- using subject experts to check the course plan for relevance and accuracy of the aims, outcomes, assessment, and content;
- using learning materials experts to check the course plan for good practice in learning materials design;
- field testing.

These are generally used in combination to tie internal self-auditing to external assessments. Professional bodies could also help monitor an institution's systems through external review. Some independent or integrated education organisations also exist to promote and support quality improvement and produce best practice guidelines or provide support networks for ODL practitioners.

Kirkpatrick (2005) has proposed that a framework for managing quality in ODL should address the following:

- *General philosophy*: Policy and mission statements, ethos and culture of the organization, mottoes, attitudes of staff, and levels of staff commitment.
- *Products*: Learning materials, courses, resources, media, outputs (progression and retention rates, number of graduates), and assessment outcomes (pass rates, standards of performance).
- *Services*: Registration and advisory services, tutoring, counseling, feedback and guidance on learning, support for learner progress, provision and management of study centers and resources, customer service, ICT help desks, and responsiveness to issues.
- *Support processes*: Delivery systems, record keeping, scheduling, electronic backup, warehousing, and stock control.

Koul and Kanwar (2006) have also analyzed quality assurance in ODL from the perspective of process-based concerns, values-based philosophy, and transaction-based pedagogic concerns.

On the issue of process-based systemic concerns the authors explain the process for assessment made up of curriculum design; course preparation, including instructional design, developmental testing, and peer review; assignment handling and turnaround time for feedback; course delivery, including student support services; student evaluation and program evaluation; and overall monitoring of the entire system, including its cost efficiency and effectiveness. All these course areas are subject to critical assessment to ensure that there is total credibility and that standards are not being compromised in any way.

A values-based philosophical concern is the assessment of the program in the national and international frameworks of education. Assessors look out for the program's ability to widen access to education and ensure equitable distribution. ODL programs should be able to meet individual, national, and international aspirations in education. The issue of gender, race, differential income levels, and other divides in society must be adequately addressed.

Transaction-based pedagogic/androgogic concerns deal with issues about the teaching-learning transaction. Like all educational enterprises ODL programs should be able to provide diverse combinations of cognitive, psychomotor, and affective domains. In assessing the content and delivery methods of ODL programs, the ability to equip an individual in all the domains is assessed.

The best way for an ODL institution to achieve high standards of quality assurance is to ensure the achievements of high standards in all its processes of operation. Standards should not be compromised in any way. As noted by Koul and Kanwar (2006) this could be achieved with proactive and innovative management, transparency in operation and financial management, investment in institution-specific systematic and regular research, investment in ICT applications, innovations in policy frameworks, administrative processes, curricular and instructional design, focus on issues of diversity, and above all the cultivation of a culture of quality assurance.

The Technology Factor

ODL thrives on technology. It is a fully mechanized system of education. Even the printed materials are processed mechanically. ICT thus forms an essential part of ODL programs. Some of the ways of using ICT in ODL have included the following

- Self-study learning materials such as workbooks, audiocassettes, videocassettes, computer programs, kits, and Web sites.
- Technology-mediated tutorials, seminars, workshops, counseling sessions, and other support systems—usually by a part-time tutor, who may also have a separate full-time job as a teacher or on the Internet.
- Synchronous communication—for example, the use of the telephone to maintain student–tutor contact.
- Asynchronous communication between students and tutors, for example, e-mails and computer conferencing.
- Assessment and accreditation—this may take a particular form to match the philosophy of the system or may follow the standard assessment system for on-campus students.

ICT permeates almost all the ODL implementation approaches listed above. The choice of technology to support the system must, however, be done with some caution.

Writers on technology for teaching and learning tend to support its use enthusiastically whenever possible and to assume that the latest technology is the best because it is usually an improvement on the former. In practice, most studies comparing one technology with another come to the conclusion that they are all equally effective.

Bates (1995, 16–17, in COL 2002) suggests that media should be chosen on the basis of six factors:

- Accessibility to students
- Costs to institution
- Teaching capability
- Capacity for interactivity
- Organizational impact
- Speed of update

Accessibility to students—Just as ODL courses seek to be highly accessible to all students without barriers, so is the expectation of the technology used in the program delivery. Students should be able to have easy access to the technology that is being used. There is no point in choosing media that your students will have difficulty accessing. Printed materials, for instance, are accessible to all students irrespective of geographical location, income level, infrastructure development, or gender. Other media to be used could depend on students having access to the appropriate technology such as radio if material is broadcast, or a computer that is connected to the Internet or has a CD-ROM drive. Finding out from existing or prospective students could be an effective way of assessing the most appropriate technology to use.

Cost to institution—The issue of cost cannot be overlooked in choosing media for an ODL program. The bottom line of the decision on media is cost. The system should be affordable to both the institution and the existing and prospective students. The high cost of technology will no doubt affect the fees to be paid by students, which could possibly limit access by the most deprived learner, who should benefit most from the program.

Teaching capability—The purpose of technology in an ODL program is for teaching. Hence the institution will have to consider the ability of the media to serve as an effective tool for teaching. COL indicates that the media mix must be able to

- stimulate/motivate learners;
- present new material;
- provoke student interaction;
- give feedback to students; and
- help students assess their progress.

Detailed illustration has been provided in Table 14.

Table 14 Students Needs and Media Capabilities

Student need	Best media	Worst media
Stimulate/motivate learners	Video and audio	Print
Present new material to be learned	Print, video, audio	Broadcasting (since students cannot control the pace or review material)
Encourage students to interact with the material	Computer-based material Web-based material	Broadcasting (since there is no pause for interaction)
Give feedback to students on their work	Computer-based material Web-based material	Any mass media, e.g. print, broadcasting
Help students to assess their progress	Print Computer-based material Web-based material	Any mass media, e.g. print, broadcasting

Source: COL 2004a

Table 14 Students Needs and Media Capabilities
Source: COL 2004a

Capacity for interactivity —The essence of technology use in an ODL program is to fill in the communication gap that is missing. Ability to participate and interact serves as a booster for ODL students. With the growing interest in computer and other electronic packages among the youth, an interactive platform could highly attract them to ODL programs. Investing in media that enhances interaction among students, students and tutors, and students and the institution could be a great facilitator of the program. Since computer and other electronic packages that facilitate interaction could be very expensive for the institution and students, other means of creating interaction could be explored. This could be consciously built into the study materials through various activities. Students could also be encouraged to use their cell phones to stay connected to each other using text messages.

Organization impact—Media use has enormous implications for the institution. Some technologies may require recruiting specialists and training staff for its usage and maintenance. Others could also require huge financial investment. All these are issues that must be critically assessed before deciding on the type of technology to support the system.

Speed of update—One characteristic of technology is the speed at which it gets dated or could be upgraded. New technologies, software, and other packages are being manufactured every day. An institution will have to take into consideration the ease with which the media could be updated so that it does not get outdated in a short time. This will save the institution a lot of money.

Some expensive media like online or electronic presentation of study materials might be capital intensive to start with but very convenient to update, whereas printed material could be relatively cheaper to start with but more expensive to update. Such factors should be assessed in a broader picture before choosing media.

The Cost Factor in ODL

One thing that bothers most people about ODL is the cost implications to the government, the delivering institution, and the student. Some people perceive it as being capital intensive compared with the conventional system of education. But ODL generally offers potential economies of scale, because although development costs of materials are high, teaching costs are low. The cost structures in open and distance learning are quite different from cost structures in conventional types of education. Generally, in face-to-face teaching, the main cost is teachers' salaries and total costs rise roughly in proportion to enrollments. In ODL, there is often a large up-front fixed cost for the development of materials and systems. This cost can be avoided to a certain extent if the system adopts certain strategies such as using ODL materials bought from other institutions. However, only a small proportion of ODL providers take this approach, suggesting that it is rarely possible to find materials that match the needs of the providers' students. Once the up-front course development costs have been met, the additional cost of teaching one more student is very low. The cost becomes limited to the marginal costs of tutoring. Much as there are strategies to cut initial costs, there is no doubt that there will also be a balance of costs for online learning. For instance, online delivery systems could have high up-front investments and possibly higher recurrent costs, since tutors may have to spend more time working with online students.

In most cases, however, open and distance learning is perceived to be more cost-efficient than other forms of education. Among the factors said to contribute to this are the use of media that enable relatively few teachers to reach very large numbers of students, the fact that some ODL systems do not need classrooms, and the very different cost structure of ODL arising from the substitution of capital in the form of teaching materials for labor.

Some of the common types of costs involved in an ODL systems are as follows:

- Fixed costs include start-up investments in office space and course development. These do not usually rise as more students are enrolled.

- Variable costs include payment to tutors and printing of instructional materials, which rise every time new students are enrolled.
- Maintenance costs are a type of fixed cost that has to be incurred on regular basis to keep the system running. An example could be staff remuneration.

In addressing the costing problem in ODL there is the argument that students in open and distance learning, who are often working adults, should pay a higher proportion of the costs than conventional students. This argument has to be handled with some level of caution. In some developing countries governments want a large proportion of expenditure to be paid by the students through school fees. Students differ from country to country and community to community. They have different income levels. Most of these ODL programs are also organized with the aim of widening access and make education affordable. So if precautions are taken, the fees could make the program miss its target. In some instances some distance learners ask for treatment similar to that of their colleagues on campus. They want access to loans and scholarship and even paid study leave facilities. The balance of funding from government, employers, and individual students should therefore be carefully considered, to remedy any unjustified economic discrimination between students in open and distance learning and on-campus students. As much as possible a standardization of the system will be useful for all.

On a general note, distance-learning programs with high enrollment levels could produce graduates at considerably lower costs than conventional institutions. This depends, however, on a number of other factors. The factors affecting the cost efficiency of open and distance learning systems include the number of students, size of the curriculum, cost of developing the instructional materials, length of usage of instructional materials before revising, choice of technology for delivery, methods of assessment, student support systems, and extent of administrative overheads.

On the issue of course development, most ODL systems involve the production of learning materials, which could result in high up-front capital costs. Because these costs have to be met before any students are enrolled, ODL can appear expensive. However, as more and more students are enrolled, unit costs fall. Buying courses from an existing institution could help reduce the unit cost.

Size of the curriculum also affects the start-up capital. The broader the curriculum on offer, the more courses that need to be offered, and the greater the volume of course materials that needs to be developed. The cost per student will therefore continue to rise unless the increase in the number of courses is taken care of by an increase in the number of students.

ODL materials are expected to be revised on a regular basis to avoid their becoming too dated. Meanwhile this could be a very expensive process for an institution. There may not be standard time lines for this. It is necessary for an institution to draw a revision plan that will not cause a financial crisis. The cost of revision could also be determined by the mode of the material. It might be less expensive to review materials that are delivered in an electronic form than those that are in printed form, for instance. Hence the decision on the mode of presentation of ODL material should take into consideration the cost of review as well.

Another way of running a cost-efficient ODL program is to look for opportunities to share the cost of production. An institution could enter into a contract with a publisher interested in publishing the material for the institution. In dual institutions, there could be the possibility of selling the modules in the school's bookstore to on-campus students. This strategy will not only help generate extra income to manage the cost, but with the quality of ODL materials this will be an opportunity to market the program among students and faculty in the entire institution as well. An institution could also form a consortium with another as a means of sharing the cost in material development.

Technology used in the program as usual has a lot of cost implications. To break even in an ODL program, an institution will have to settle on a technology based on its cost-benefit analysis. Therefore the choice of technology should be based on its user-friendliness, student affordability, and accessibility, but the cost implications to the institution must be a key factor.

Support for students at a distance is central to the delivery of ODL, but it can also be very expensive if not well managed. Much as an institution may not have to "cut corners" in the provision of support to students, there should be cost analysis in deciding on the extent and nature of support services for them. Support should be just what students need to be able to stay in the program and make good grades. A good performance will no doubt attract more students to the program, which will in turn add to the income of the program.

Above all, an ODL institution will have to make a conscious effort to manage its resources and administrative overheads in such a way that expenditures will constantly be lower than income. If the program is well managed, fees charged could also be affordable and attractive to a wide range of male and female students, especially in the developing world, and thus increase enrollment levels as well. A massive marketing drive and quality in operations, which will definitely affect students' performances, will also be a sure way of constantly keeping the program in good financial standing.

The Management Factor

Management remains a critical factor in the success and sustainability of an ODL program. ODL programs need effective and efficient administration that will ensure the smooth running of the program. As an industrialized form of teaching, well-established and integrated systems are required in managing ODL programs. Staff development, quality assurance, and support staff form essential components in the management of an ODL system.

Staff development—Being a relatively new enterprise, the people recruited to work on an ODL program will require some specialized skills to be able to do a good job. They have to be given the necessary orientation and training and constantly monitored on the job to ensure that work flows well in a professional manner. Management has the task of developing the capacity of staff upon hiring and regularly on the job to achieve high performance.

Quality assurance—The only way to improve the performance of students and help remove the "inferiority tag" on an ODL program is to ensure quality in all its processes. Quality assurance processes begins with the staff recruitment stage and goes through to the development of instructional materials, provision of support systems, tutoring, and assessment of students. Management has no business compromising on standards in an ODL program. Hence they have the task of paying close attention to quality assurance.

Support staff—As an industrialized system of education, the success of an ODL program depends not only on the course writers but rather the role of the people who:

- go to the office early to clean and might possibly meet and take the queries of students who pass by the school on their way to work;
- sit at the front desk to welcome or take students' queries on the phone;
- compile student records, including examination scores;
- process instructional materials; and
- distribute modules and fliers.

These are all very critical. Good planning, orientation, training, appreciable remuneration packages, and a culture of information sharing cannot be overlooked. The management of an ODL institution should not take operations or any staff for granted.

The development of instructional materials, student support systems, the role of the tutor, finance, media, assessments of students, and effective management all form essential components of an ODL system. An effective administrative system has the task of managing all these components in a professional manner. This way one will be working toward absolute quality in an ODL program.

Chapter 7

The Practice of Distance Education in Ghana

The mission of distance education programs in Ghana is to make high-quality education at all levels more accessible and relevant, meeting the needs of Ghanaians to enhance their performance and improve the quality of their lives. Specifically government of Ghana have sought to use distance education to

- provide opportunity for a large number of qualified applicants who are not admitted into the face-to-face programs as a result of limited facilities to have access to tertiary education;
- create the opportunity for work and study;
- increase access to and participation in education at all levels for all;
- facilitate progression through the education system from basic to tertiary;
- improve the capacity of Ghanaians to cope with technological advancement and the knowledge society and be able to enhance their contribution to nation building;
- increase equality and democratisation of education;

- provide cost-effective and affordable education; and
- serve as an avenue for financial resource mobilization for the public universities.

For decades the country was faced with having to turn away a large number of qualified applicants every year because of the limited space available, especially at the tertiary level of education. The government of Ghana then planned to use distance education to respond to the growing demands for tertiary education in the country and to decongest the campuses of the public universities. After this, distance education centers were established in four public universities: the University of Ghana (UG), Kwame Nkrumah University of Science and Technology (KNUST), the University of Cape Coast (UCC), and the University of Education, Winneba (UEW) to manage and support distance education. Out of these public universities, the distance education program was first begun in UEW in the year 1996, followed by UCC in 2001, then KNUST in 2004, and finally UG in 2007. Before then, in collaboration with the Commonwealth of Learning, the University of Ghana had been delivering a Diploma in Youth in Development Work since 2001. Historical records also show that the Institute of Adult Education of the University of Ghana delivered correspondence courses for workers for General Certificate Examination in the 1970s.

The government of Ghana has thus adopted distance education as a viable complement to conventional face-to-face education. The four public universities have become dual-mode institutions to deliver both on-campus and distance learning programs. This chapter focuses on the various distance learning programs on offer by the institutions, delivery approaches, administrative arrangements, and other aspects of the programs.

Operation of Distance Education Ghana

The delivery of distance education is not new in the country. Distance education delivery in Ghana dates back to the correspondence era in the 1960s, when some Ghanaians sought certificates for clerical and other "white collor" jobs. Thus correspondence courses with Wolsey College, Rapid Results College, Mayflower College, and the U.S.–based International Correspondence School among others provided the opportunity for several workers to upgrade themselves (Ansere 2002; Aggor and Kinyanjui 1992; Kwapong 2007; Kwapong 2008d). There was also the Modular Teacher Training Program (MTTP), introduced in 1982 to upgrade untrained teachers academically and professionally. This program enabled 7,537 untrained teachers to receive professional training and to qualify for Teachers' Certificate "A" (Mensah and Owusu-Mensah 2002).

In addition to the promotion of distance learning in the public universities and for professional development, there has been a President's Special Initiative on Distance Learning (PSIDL 2002). The PSIDL was launched in April 2002 and revealed the government's reaffirmation of its policy of using distance education to improve the quality of education at all levels. The purpose of the PSIDL is to examine how technology could be used to improve the quality of education in the country at the basic secondary and teacher-training levels. Further, the initiative seeks to establish an open college. A fifteen-member committee has since been appointed to implement the initiative. Since its inauguration the committee has been working on a pilot project that uses television to teach mathematics and English to junior high school and senior high school students.

Overview of the Tertiary Distance Education (DE) Programs

The four universities that have started DE programs (UG, KNUST, UCC, and UEW) are now dual-mode institutions.

As a practice for parity of esteem and standardization, the institutions use the same faculty, curriculum, course structure, and content for both the on-campus and the distance education students. The admission and examination process is similar for both sets of students. Similar matriculation and graduation programs are organized for both sets of students as well. The delivery mode at a distance has been predominantly print-based supported with regular face-to-face programs at the various learning centers. Whereas some institutions conduct both mid-semester and end-of-semester assessments at their centers in the regions, others do it at a central point, usually the main campus of the university.

The government of Ghana seeks to ensure quality in its distance education programs. This is to be done by decreasing the dropout rate and improving learner achievement and retention, producing independent and autonomous learners, building the technical skills of all staff who work on distance learning programs, ensuring parity in both the on-campus and the distance learning programs, and assuring quality in all the distance education processes.

In the area of governance, managers and stakeholders of ODL programs work to provide direction for the effective implementation of ODL programs in the country, and develop and implement systems for monitoring and evaluation.

With funding support from the World Bank through the Teaching and Learning Innovation Fund, the Ghana Education Trust Fund, and other funding agencies, the National Council for Tertiary Education (NCTE) has been able to provide infrastructural and capacity-building support to the ongoing ODL programs. The various distance education institutions have been able to acquire basic facilities such as computers, Internet connectivity, libraries, refurbishing of learning centers in the regions, and other infrastructural and logistical support. Training support over the years has been received from both local and international institutions such as the NCTE, Ministry of Education Science and

Sports, International Extension College of the United Kingdom and Simon Frazer University Distance Education Centre of Canada, British Overseas Development Administration (ODA), and the Commonwealth of Learning in the areas of writing, formatting, and editing of instructional materials, learner support services, and general administration and management of DE programs. These supports have been very useful in building local capacity and expertise.

There have been modest attempts to utilize ICT potentials in the ongoing programs. There are attempts to use radio stations that serve the various university communities and their immediate environs for promotion of the distance learning programs and even in some cases provide tutor support. A case is the use of an FM station at UCEW to deliver lectures to large classes, which offers an innovative opportunity for the inclusion of radio as a teaching medium (Centre for Continuing Education 2006; UEW 2006; UG 2007; Mensah and Owusu-Mensah 2002). Table 15 presents an overview of the status of the tertiary distance education programs, followed by a discussion of some specifics of the various institutions.

Table 15 Profile of Distance Education Programs in Ghana

Name of University	University of Education Winneba	University of Cape Coast	Kwame Nkrumah University of Science and Tech	University of Ghana
Name of Distance Education Department	Institute for Educational Development and Extension—Centre for Distance Education	Centre for Continuing Education	Institute of Distance Learning	Centre for Distance Education
Year Established	1993	1997	-	-
Year DE Prog. Began	1996	2001	2004	2007
Number of Students Began	196	709	30	959
Current Enrollment	9,284 (as of October 2008)	18,423 (as of March 2006)	2,500	
Courses on Offer	Basic Education	Basic Education Business Management Management and Administration of Basic Schools	Computer Engineering Quantity Survey and Construction Construction Technology and Management Sociology Social Work Industrial Mathematics Environmental Science Post-Harvest Technology Business Admin.	Economics Geography Linguistics Psychology History Sociology Social Work Business Admin.
Certificates to Obtain	3-Year Diploma in Basic 2-Year Post-Diploma Degree (B.ED in Basic Education)	Diploma in Basic Education (DBE) Post-Diploma Degree in Basic Education (P-DBE) Diploma in Commerce/ Management Stds Post-Dip. In Commerce/Mgt Stds Master's Degree in Management and Administration of Basic Schools	BSc. Computer Engineering BSc. Quantity Survey and Construction BSc. Construction Technology and Management BA Sociology and Social Work MSc Industrial Mathematics MSc Environmental Science MSc Post-Harvest Technology MSc—EMBA, EMPA (CDL)	BA (Arts) BA Administration (Accounting/Mgt.) BSc. Administration

Table 15 Profile of Distance Education Programs in Ghana

University of Education, Winneba

The UEW established the Institute for Educational Development and Extension (IEDE) in 1993. The IEDE, which is responsible for the delivery of DE in UEW, was established in the second year of the university's existence. This initiated the provision of a tertiary distance education program that provides dual-mode programs in Ghana. Since its establishment, DE has been a prominent part of UEW programs. The founding of the institute coincided with the decision of the British Overseas Development Administration (ODA) to support quality improvement of education in Ghana in accordance with the Educational Reform Program by assisting with the production of trained teachers for primary, junior, and senior high schools as well as initial training colleges. Until 2001, the University of Education, Winneba, through IEDE, was the only university in Ghana that offered distance learning as part of its core programs. IEDE provides access to quality teacher education for all teachers who want to upgrade themselves. The mission of IEDE is to provide leadership in the development, provision, and maintenance of effective extension services in education to prepare teachers, educational professionals, and people from other professions and industries for service to the nation. The institute seeks to provide greater access to higher education in a much more efficient manner with the application of better equipment and human resources at the institute and various study centers in the ten regions of the country.

The distance education program of the institute is in line with the university's mission to equip teachers with the requisite academic proficiency and professional competency for teaching at the pre-tertiary level. The institute was established to deliver distance learning programs with particular reference to teachers, recognizing that about 15,000 Certificate "A" teachers leave the classroom each year for further studies, creating vacancies that are difficult to fill. This situation affects teaching and learning (Mensah and Owusu-Mensah 2002). The DE program of the institute gives teachers the opportunity to remain in the classroom and offer their services while upgrading themselves.

The DE program of IEDE focuses on teacher education, with the same academic and professional components as the on-campus programs. The academic component comprises specific subjects taught in primary/secondary schools and colleges (such as mathematics and social studies). The professional component, on the other hand, consists of the theory of education, school management, and pedagogy. The DE program has thus been in line with the university's mission to equip teachers with the requisite academic proficiency and professional competency for teaching at the pre-tertiary level.

Recognizing that ODL suits the learning-and lifestyle of women, the institute has been making a conscious effort to admit female students into the program. As a result of this effort, women formed 54 percent of the institute's first four batches of enrollment from 1998 to 2002. The trend of higher female enrollment continues in current available enrollment data. This has allowed the institute to continue being a leading institution in making DE accessible to women. The most current available data shows that in October 2008 66 percent of the first-year students were females. For its Level 300 (2004) year group, Level 200 (2006) year group, and Level 300 (2006) year group, female enrollment continues to be on the high side as presented in Figures 14 to 17. Figures 14 to 17 indicate the relatively high percentage of female enrollment over the period.

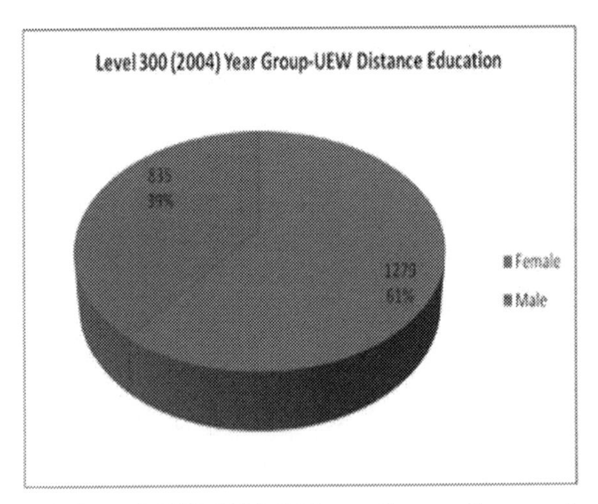

Figure 14 Level 300 (2004) Year Group Source: Institute for Educational Development and Extension (IEDE) 2006

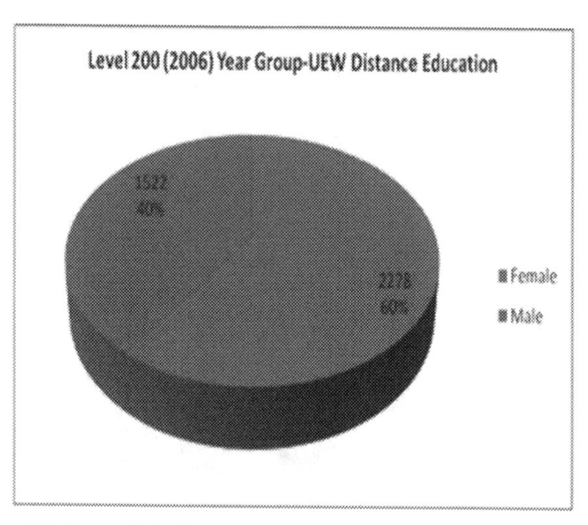

Figure 15 Level 200 (2006) Year Group Source: Institute for Educational Development and Extension (IEDE) 2006

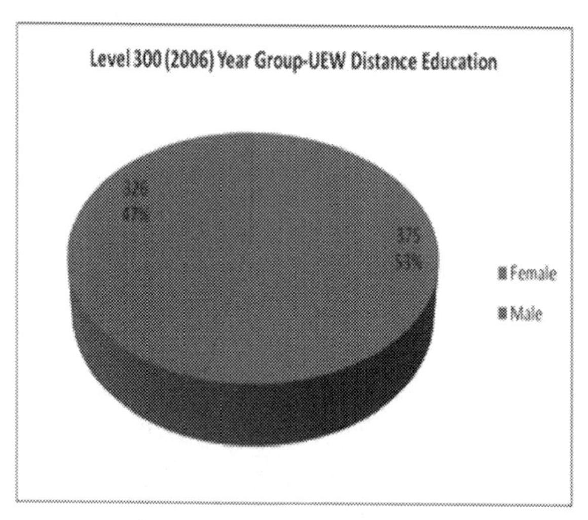

Figure 16 Level 300 (2006) Year Group Source: Institute for Educational Development and Extension (IEDE) 2006

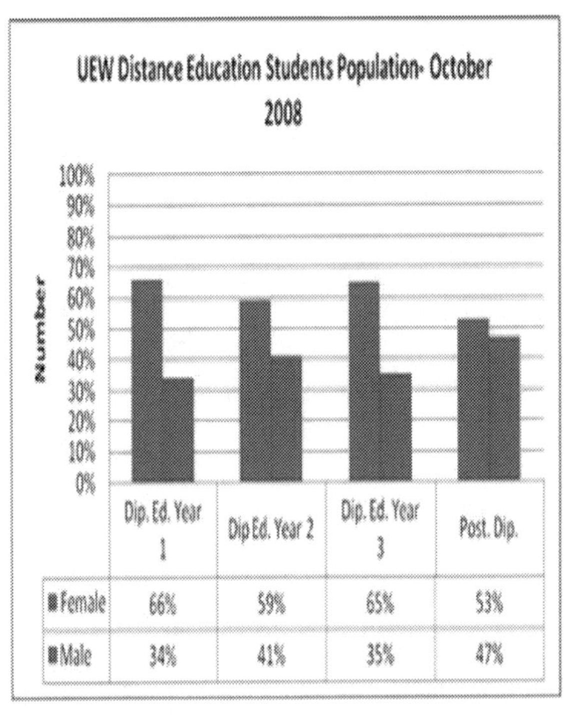

Figure 17 Student Population for 2008/2009

Source: Institute for Educational Development and Extension (IEDE) 2009

The support services available to students include the following:

- Study centers
- Orientation sessions at the start of each academic year
- Monthly face-to-face tutorials at the study centers
- Provision of student handbooks and study materials
- Academic progress feedback through tutor-marked assignments

University of Cape Coast

University of Cape Coast established the Centre for Continuing Education (CCE) in 1997 to mount all viable programs of the university in distance mode and thereby provide greater access to tertiary education in Ghana. Specifically, CCE is to train more professional (basic school) teachers for the basic education level to upgrade their academic and professional competence. The center also operates to raise the professional competence and qualifications of serving personnel in public service, industry, and commerce for accelerated national development. The center has, since October 2001, pursued this mandate effectively by mounting seven programs at the diploma, post-diploma degree, and master's levels.

The student population of the center has increased significantly over the years. From a modest beginning of 709 students in the 2001/2002 academic year, the center's student population reached about 12,000 students in the 2005/2006 academic year with an appreciable female enrollment as indicated in Figures 18, 19, and 20.

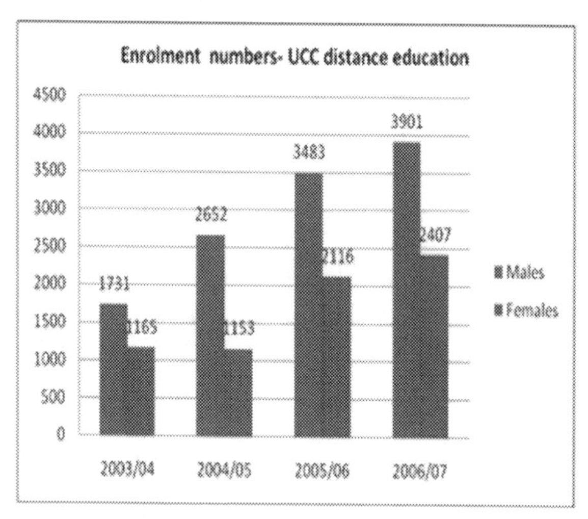

Figure 18 Enrollment Statistics—2003–2007 Source: Centre for Continuing Education

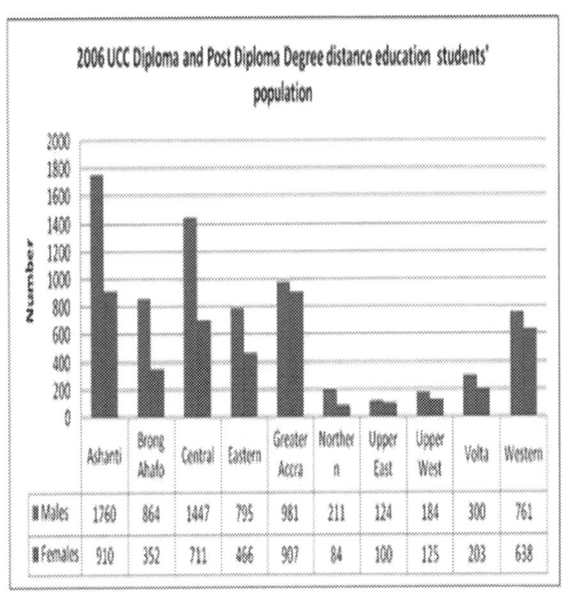

	Ashanti	Brong Ahafo	Central	Eastern	Greater Accra	Northern	Upper East	Upper West	Volta	Western
Males	1760	864	1447	795	981	211	124	184	300	761
Females	910	352	711	466	907	84	100	125	203	638

Figure 19 Enrollment Statistics—2006 Only

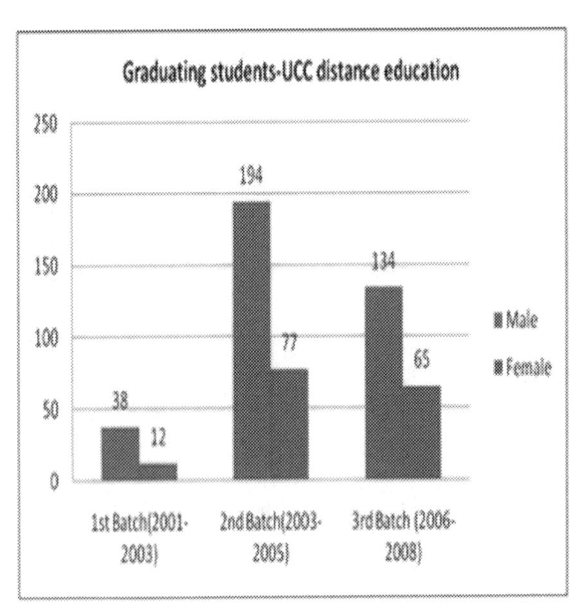

Figure 20 Graduating Students 2001–2008 Source: Centre for Continuing Education 2008

The number of study centers has consistently increased from nine in 2001/2002 to thirty study centers throughout the country to correspond to the increase in student numbers.

Assessment of a student's performance is made by a combination of continuous assessment and an end-of-semester examination. Continuous assessment is based on the student's performance on tutor-marked assignments and quizzes throughout the course. This might have informed the low student dropout rate. Table 16 provides the completion and dropout percentages over the period.

Table 16 Students Completion and Dropout Rates: Diploma in Basic Education Program (2001–2007)

Year	No. Offered Admission	No. Enrolled	No. Completed	No. Dropout	% Completed	% Dropout
2001 – 2003	721	651	630	21	96.8	3.2
2002 – 2004	2,522	2,346	2,274	72	96.9	3.1
2003 – 2005	2,864	2,563	2,471	94	96.4	3.6
2004 – 2006	2,963	2,829	2,718	111	96.1	3.9
2005 – 2007	3,009	2,445	2,316	129	94.5	5.5
Total	12,079	10,834	7,691	427	96.14	3.86

Source: Centre for Continuing Education 2008

Table 16 Students Completion and Dropout Rates: Diploma in Basic Education Program (2001–2007) Source: Centre for Continuing Education 2008

The support services available to students consist of

- study centers,
- tutoring/counseling,
- orientation of freshmen,
- residential sessions,
- library services, and
- information sharing.

Kwame Nkrumah University of Science and Technology

The Kwame Nkrumah University of Science and Technology started its distance learning program in the 2004/2005 academic year to offer some of its programs at a distance.

Since its beginning, the student population of the program has increased significantly. The program began with thirty students in the 2004/2005 academic year and has increased to a population of 2,500.

Assessment of the students consists of assignments and quizzes (25 percent), and attendance at tutorials (5 percent), and examinations (70 percent). Delivery is basically done face-to-face and online.

University of Ghana

The distance education program of the University of Ghana took off in 2007. The Centre for Distance Education started with 959 in 2007, enrolled 1,787 students in the 2008/2009 academic year, and has set a goal of 2,500 freshmen for its 2009/2010 academic year.

The study centers are at the regional center of the Institute of Adult Education. The study centers, which provide physical facilities such as classrooms, are used for tutoring and counseling, discussion groups, and storing and distributing study materials. Students are assessed by a written end-of-semester examination.

The Figure 21 below shows the number of Level 100 and Level 200 students per study center.

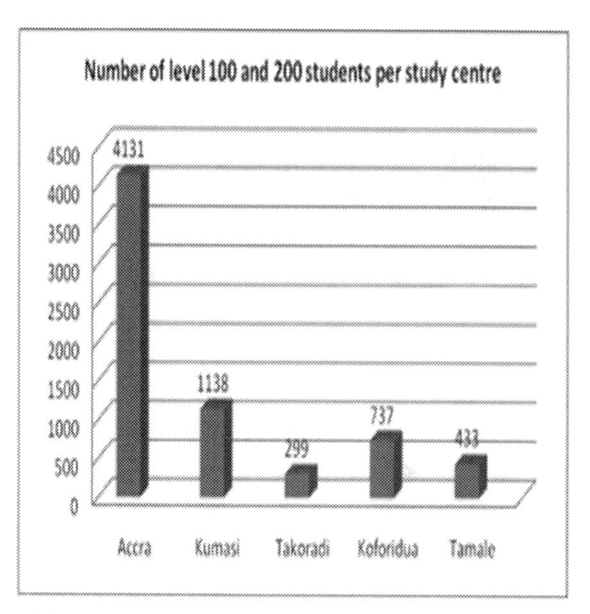

Figure 21 Enrollments of Levels 100 and 200 Students per Study Center Source: University of Ghana (UG) 2007

Support services available to students are

- study center support,
- tutoring/counseling,
- residential sessions,
- library services, and
- information sharing.

Issues to Consider

The review of the tertiary distance education programs raises several issues of concern. It is exciting to know that the various programs are providing an opportunity for tertiary education for people who, though qualified, might not have had the opportunity to pursue it. An institution such as IEDE has made a conscious effort to enroll more women, which has contributed to increased female enrollment in the program. Available reports also indicate that IEDE is making an effort to use ICT facilities such as radio to complement delivery. The programs are thus helping to promote equitable access to education at the tertiary level.

However, there are challenges that have to be considered for a better equitable provision of tertiary education.

To date, print continues to be the medium most used by the various institutions offering distance education. This has been complemented with some electronic media such as online resources, CD copies of the instructional materials, and course Web sites for effective communication and interaction among tutors and students, administrators and students, and the students themselves.

A unifying body and an effective collaboration between the various institutions could facilitate the sharing of both academic and ICT infrastructural resources.

Part 3 ODL and ICT for Women

Chapter 8

ICT Knowledge and Usage among Distance Learners

In view of the improvement in the provision of information and communication technology (ICT) facilities and services, a study was conducted to determine the nature of ICT knowledge and usage among 626 distance learners from all ten regions in the country. The study was mainly based on access to the Internet and usage and ownership of personal computers. Usage of the Internet and ownership of computers is emphasized because of the advantages they bring, such as access to vast data sources and possible interactivity. The results of the survey give an indication of the extent of utilization of ICT facilities among the students in their private day-to-day activities so that one can be sure of their possible exposure to and capabilities of using such ICT facilities for educational purposes at a distance.

Profile of the Study Areas

Ghana has ten administrative regions. The study covered all ten. The economic activities, educational infrastructure, literacy levels, and most important, availability of telecommunication facilities in the ten regions have been assessed in this section with information from the Ministry of Local Government and Rural Development (MLGRD 2006) and the Ghana Living Standards Survey 4 (GLSS 4 2000). The educational and ICT profile of the country has been discussed in earlier sections. This review helps undertake a detailed assessment of the situation in the various regions and their in-depth peculiarities. The review of the regional demographics shows that there are variations in terms of infrastructural development, most especially in telecommunication. As a reflection of national statistics, literacy levels are not all that high; access to educational facilities is not high at the higher level of education. Agriculture is the main source of income for most of the regions.

Postal services have been moderately available in all regions. However, the provision of fixed lines to the regions has not been progressive enough. Rather, mobile telephony is providing telecommunication services in most of the regions. Availability of Internet facilities is also not predominant in the regional data that was accessed. There is limited access to electricity in most of the districts, which is a core factor in the use of ICT facilities. Some regions indicated the use of solar energy, but it appears to be on a pilot basis rather than being regionwide. One should note, however, that the source of information could be so dated that it may not be a full representation of the current situation, especially when there is rapid growth in ICT facilities. The information provided could give an idea of how the situation has once been. Detailed profiles of the various regions have been provided below[1].

Ashanti Region

The Ashanti region occupies a total land area of 24,389 square kilometers representing 10.2 percent of the total land area of

1 For more detailed information on all the regions and districts in Ghana visit www.ghanadistricts.com/home/.

Ghana. It is the third largest region after the Northern (70,384 sq. kms) and Brong Ahafo (39,557 sq. kms) regions. There are twenty-seven administrative districts in the Ashanti Region, including the Kumasi metropolis. The economically active population in the region is engaged mainly in agriculture (excluding fishing), with 44.5 percent of workers employed in other economic activities.

Information on the levels of educational attainment and literacy show that between 40 and 50 percent of the population in the region, particularly females, either have no formal education or have only pre-school education. Available data reveals that 35 percent of the population fifteen years and older in the region are not literate. A little less than half (48.1 percent) are literate in both English and a Ghanaian language. Only 3.2 percent are literate in a Ghanaian language only, and less than 1 percent are able to read and write in other languages. There are differences between the sexes in terms of literacy. More than half (55.8 percent) of the males are literate in English and a Ghanaian language compared with two-fifths (40.4 percent) of the females. On the whole, the illiteracy level for the region (35 percent) is lower than that of the national average (42.1 percent). Illiteracy levels are high in the districts and higher for females than the males. The level is also higher in rural areas than in urban areas. There are 330 kindergartens in the metropolis, of which 239 are privately owned. At the primary school level, the private sector has 269 schools, whereas the public sector has 179. However, at the Junior Secondary School level, the public sector leads with 137 schools, compared with the private sector's 84 schools. There are thirty second-cycle institutions in the metropolis, comprising senior secondary schools, commercial, technical, and vocational institutions, and training colleges. The metropolis has three major tertiary institutions: the Kwame Nkrumah University of Science and Technology, the Kumasi Polytechnic, and a campus of the University College of Education.

Kerosene is the main source of fuel used for lighting in fifteen of the eighteen districts. The regional capital, Kumasi, is by far the largest electricity local center. Most parts of the metropolis have electricity supply, although demand exceeds supply capabilities.

Two types of telecommunication networks exist in Kumasi: the mobile networks and the fixed-line system, as in any other modern city. There is only one operator for the fixed-line system in Kumasi, Ghana Telecommunications Company Limited (Vodaphone). However, there are four operators for the mobile telecommunications network system: Ghana Telecommunications Company Limited (Vodaphone), Scancom Ghana Limited, Millicom Ghana Limited, and Celltell Communications Group. With the mobile network there is some variety and access is fairly easy. However, with the fixed-line system there is some form of monopoly, as only Ghana Telecommunications Company Limited (Vodaphone) provides the service.

Brong Ahafo Region

Brong Ahafo has nineteen administrative districts. The region has a population of 1,815,408. Agriculture and related work is the major occupation in all districts, accounting for 66.4 percent of the region's economically active population. Significant proportions of the economically active people are engaged in production, or as transport operators, laborers (11.3 percent), sales workers (7.6 percent), and professional and related workers (5.8 percent). The private informal sector provides employment to about four out of every five members of the workforce in the region.

More than two-fifths (42 percent) of the population aged six and older have never been to school. The proportion of the population not literate (48.5 percent) in the region is higher than the national average (42.1 percent). The region has 769 Junior

Secondary Schools and 60 senior secondary schools. There are three teacher-training colleges in the region and twenty-four technical, commercial, and vocational institutions, all privately owned, as well as three specialized schools and one polytechnic.

There is a correlation between urbanization and the use of electricity. For all the districts with more than half the population living in the urban areas, electricity is the main source of lighting. The kerosene lamp (63.6 percent) and electricity (35.5 percent) are the main sources of lighting for households in all districts. Solar energy is the least-used source of lighting, and is used in only three districts, Berekum, Nkoranza and Tano, where just 0.1 percent of the households use it. All districts have postal agencies as well. All the district capitals apart from three are connected to Ghana Telecom lines. Two mobile phone services, MTN and Vodaphone, are available in the region.

Central Region

The Central Region's population is 1,593,823. It has twelve administrative districts. The predominant industry in all districts except Cape Coast is agriculture (52.3 percent), followed by manufacturing (10.5 percent).

Among those in the region fifteen and older, 57.1 percent are literate. This figure is almost the same as the national average of 57.9 percent. Most of the literate (37 percent) can read and write in both English and a Ghanaian language. Another 16.6 percent of the population is literate in English only. There are more males literate (69.8 percent) than there are females (46.3 percent), and the numbers are similar in all districts. The region has 1,207 primary schools, 856 Junior Secondary Schools, and 49 senior secondary schools. It boasts some of the best secondary schools in the country and is endowed with two universities.

The main sources of lighting in the region are electricity (40.1 percent) and kerosene (58.9 percent), with kerosene being used more widely. Very few communities in the region have post offices. There are only thirty post offices and fifty-four postal agencies in the region. The distribution of telephone facilities is not different from that of post offices. With the exception of Cape Coast, less than 10 percent of localities in the other districts have telephone facilities within the communities. There is, however, a relatively higher coverage of mobile telephony.

Eastern Region

The Eastern region, with an area of 19,323 square kilometers, occupying 8.1 percent of the total land area of Ghana, is the sixth largest region of the country. The region has a total population of 2,106,696, representing 11.1 percent of Ghana's population. It is the third most populous region after the Ashanti and Greater Accra. The population is made up of 49.2 percent males and 50.8 percent females, giving a ratio of 96.8 males to 100 females. The main occupations of the economically active population in the region are agriculture and related work (54.8 percent), sales (14.3 percent), production, transport and equipment work (14 percent), and professional and technical work (6.9 percent), with services accounting for 5 percent.

Nearly two-thirds (63.6 percent) of the population aged fifteen and older are literate; 46.4 percent are literate in both English and a Ghanaian language. The proportion of illiteracy is 36.4 percent of the regional population. The level of literacy is higher for males (73.5 percent) than for females (54.4 percent).

The kerosene lamp is the main source of lighting in the region, used by 64.3 percent of households. Apart from the kerosene lamp, electricity is the second major source of lighting, in 34.3 percent of households.

Greater Accra Region

The Greater Accra Region is the smallest of the ten administrative regions in terms of area, occupying a total land surface of 3,245 square kilometers or 1.4 percent of the total land area of Ghana. In terms of population, it is the second most populated region, after the Ashanti region, with a population of 2,905,726 in 2000, accounting for 15.4 percent of Ghana's total population.

Economic activities of the people are not predominantly agriculture but rather sales and service (42 percent), professional, technical, and related workers (10.8 percent), and others.

Unlike all the other regions, literacy is relatively high here (78.2 percent). The proportion of males at the senior high school, vocational/technical, and tertiary levels in all the districts is much higher than it is for females. However, the reverse is the case for people at the non-tertiary post-secondary (teacher training, nursing, agricultural extension) level. The proportions are 47.7 percent in English and a Ghanaian language, 23.8 percent in English only, 5.6 percent in Ghanaian language only, and 1.1 percent in other languages. The literacy rate ranges from 39.5 percent in the more rural Dangme East to 82 percent in the wholly urban Accra Metropolitan Assembly. In all the districts, the proportion of literate males is higher than that of literate females.

Infrastructure development is relatively high in this region. Electricity is used by more than three-quarters of households for lighting. Post office facilities range from 1.3 percent to 8.8 percent.

Telephone service is available in all the districts. In the Accra Metropolitan Area, telephone facility is available in all the communities and the distance to the nearest facility is less than one kilometer. Again as the national capital the region is covered by all the telephone companies in the country. The average tele-density for Greater Accra is 3.2 per 100 people, about five times that of the national average (0.7), indicating that most of the fixed-line and mobile telephones of the country are concentrated in the region. All seven of Ghana's telephone companies operate in the region.

Northern Region

Being the largest of the ten regions of the country in terms of landmass, the Northern Region occupies 70,384 square kilometers, which account for 29.5 percent of the total land area of Ghana. The population represents 9.6 percent of the country's total.

The level of educational attainment in the region is low. The highest educational level of the majority of the people is primary school for 43.6 percent of males and 53.5 percent of females. Only 22 percent of the population fifteen years and older is classified as literate. With this low level of literacy, general interest in ICT protocols in the region could be very low. The level of education has affected economic activities as well. Agriculture, hunting, and forestry are the main economic activities in the region. Thus the majority of the people operate in the informal sector, which leads to a high incidence of poverty in the region (Ghana 2003).

Compared with other parts of the country, the infrastructure development is low. Kerosene lamps are the major source of lighting, and 22 percent of households use electricity. This low electricity coverage could no doubt influence access to Internet facilities, television and radio, and other information that may have a direct effect on health, education, economic, and other developmental activities. There is also a limited availability of post office services in the region. Because of the lack of an information technology network backbone, access to phones in the region is very limited. There is, however, relatively good mobile telephony coverage.

Upper East Region

The population of the Upper East Region is primarily rural (84.3 percent) and scattered in dispersed settlements. Only 15.7 percent of the population live in urban areas. The majority of the people live in huts built of mud and roofed with straw or corrugated iron sheets. Illiteracy is 78.1 percent. As a result the majority of the population operate in the informal sector such as agriculture and related work (65.9 percent), production and transport equipment work (14.5 percent), and others.

Infrastructure development that could facilitate the provision of ICT services is minimal in the region. Postal services are available only in large settlements. Linkages of district capitals are poor and in some cases are not operational. About thirteen towns are on the national electricity grid. There are some private communication centers that serve some communities. Phones per 100 people number 0.1 in the region. There is access to some mobile telephone networks.

Upper West Region

The Upper West Region has only 17.5 percent of its total population living in urban localities. Regarding education, 69.8 percent of the population aged six and older have never attended school, and 73.9 percent of this 69.8 percent are females. The majority of the educated population—68.9 percent—completed primary and middle/Junior Secondary School. Just like the two other regions in the north, the major occupations in the region are agriculture and related work (72 percent), production and transport equipment work (12.1 percent), sales work (5.2 percent), service work (4 percent), and professional, technical, and related work (4 percent).

Infrastructure development in the region is not very much different from the other two regions, which will make their access to and utilization of ICT facilities minimal.

Volta Region

The Volta Region's population in 2000 was 1,635,421. This implies an increase of 35 percent over the 1984 count of 1,211,907, giving an annual growth rate of 1.9 percent. About 72.4 percent of the population fifteen years and older in the region (693,791) are economically active, with more females (366,564) than males (331,188). Of the economically active population, 92.3 percent are employed in various economic activities and 7.7 percent are unemployed. Workers in the agriculture, animal husbandry, fishing, and hunting sectors constitute the largest occupational groups in all the districts. A significant proportion (15.2 percent) of the economically active are employed in wholesale and retail trade.

Primary schools constitute the largest proportion of educational facilities in the district (56 percent), followed by the JHS (34.5 percent) and the SHS (9.5 percent). Improved access to education is reflected in the high adult literacy rate (58.3 percent). The male literacy level (68.7 percent) in the region is higher than the national average of 66.4 percent for males, whereas that of the females (49.1 percent) is almost the same as the national average of 49.8 percent.

The kerosene lamp is the main source of lighting in many households in every district in the region, ahead of electricity. Gas lamps are not common in any of the districts, and solar energy as a source of lighting is rarely used.

The Volta Region is not very well endowed with telecommunication facilities. Ghana Telecom's fixed landline telephone system serves the region, as well as the various mobile telephone companies. Tele-density for the region is the lowest in the country (0.1 per 100 people), a position it shares with Brong

Ahafo, the Northern, and the Upper East regions. The national average is 0.7, compared with 3.2 per 100 people for Greater Accra. The mobile or cell phone as a telecommunication facility is also available in the region. Scancom, operator of the MTN mobile system, operates from seven of the company's seventy-six nationwide locations. Ghana Telecom's One Touch mobile service also operates in the region.

Western Region

The Western Region covers an area of approximately 21,391 square kilometers, which is about 10 percent of Ghana's total land area. The four major occupations in the region are not different from the national trend. Agriculture is the predominant occupation of the economically active population in the region, accounting for about 60 percent of the regional GDP, and employs about 57 percent of the total labor force. There are more females (59.5 percent) than males (56.7 percent) in agriculture (including hunting and fishing). Production and transport work (14.5 percent), sales work (10.2 percent), and professional and technical work (5 percent) follow in that order.

The Western Region has seen some improvements in educational attainment and enrollment rates at the basic level. For instance, more than 70 percent of the population in most districts has attained basic education (primary and junior secondary/middle school). Beyond junior secondary, enrollment and attainment levels are not very encouraging. In terms of literacy, apart from Shama-Ahanta East (29.3 percent) and Wassa West (37.4 percent), which recorded relatively low levels of illiteracy, all the districts have levels much higher than the regional average of 45.7 percent. The main sources of lighting are kerosene lamp and electricity. Between them they provide lighting for about 99 percent of the households in the region.

Households in 36 percent of localities in the Shama-Ahanta East metropolis have access to a post office within the locality, and an additional 30.3 percent access one within ten kilometers.

The situation with access to telephones in the Western Region is not any better than that of post offices. Of the 12,850 fixed lines in the region as of 2000, 11,046 or 86 percent serve the Shama-Ahanta East metropolis. Of the eleven districts, only six have fixed-line telephone transmission facilities provided by Ghana Telecom. Some of the other districts are served by radiotelephone and other systems from private companies such as Capital Telecommunications. Indeed it appears as if Tarkwa is about the only town that is very well served by all the telecommunications systems in the country, perhaps because of the mining companies, which require several different types of communications systems for efficient operation.

The report from the region shows that a new but very significant phenomenon that has assumed considerable importance in telecommunication in Ghana in recent times is the mobile or cell phone. This, and Internet facilities in a rapidly growing number of Internet cafés all over the country, are beginning to have a modest but significant impact on ICT in Ghana. The Western Region is one of the regions where cell or mobile phones are beginning to impact telecommunications significantly. The region is one of the most extensively covered by the various mobile telephone operators, probably because of the high usage by the mining and other industries in the region. The region has the second highest location coverage by Scancom Ltd., operators of MTN, the largest mobile telephone system in the country.

Overall, the regional data has revealed some serious shortfalls in the availability of infrastructure, most especially electricity, telephony, Internet access, and other ICT-related facilities. Much as one may say the information is dated and therefore might not reflect the current condition, the situation might not be all that encouraging at the district or rural community levels. One anticipates that with the government's policy on ICT for Accelerated Development and the ICT for Education, the nation will improve its electricity, telephone coverage, and Internet connectivity.

In spite of the limited availability of ICT infrastructure and resources, one could still argue that the few that are available should be fully utilized, especially for educational purposes through distance learning. Just as the Western Region records that the region is one of the most extensively covered by the various mobile telephone operators, probably because of the high usage by the mining and other industries, a conscious effort to utilize the limited available resource for educational purposes could boost or facilitate the further development of ICT facilities.

The survey report discussed below shows the ICT knowledge and usage of students of the University of Ghana's Distance Education program. The study helps to find out how both male and female students are using the limited ICT resources available in their communities.

Survey Methodology

The survey sought to find out the ICT situation most specifically with reference to knowledge and usage in all ten regions. The population for the study was distance learners who are scattered all over the country. The learners were pursuing a first degree program. The purpose was simply to test the knowledge and usage of basic ICT facilities such as the Internet and search engines like Google, to find out about the ownership of ICT facilities, and to discover how much the students who were users invest and are willing to further invest in such services to support their studies at a distance.

The survey instrument was structured to cover demographics of the respondents, including sex, age, level of education, household size, and marital status. Other sections of the instrument covered knowledge of ICT and search engines, frequency of usage, purpose of usage, and fees paid for usage. Willingness to own a personal computer and payment of fees for usage of an Internet service was also investigated. Specific questions included the following: Do you know what ICT is? Do you use the Internet? Where do you access the Internet? How long on average do you stay on the Internet? How many times per week do you use the café? How much do you pay per hour? What do you use the Internet for? Do you know that the Internet could be used to access educational materials? Are you aware of search engines such as Google that you can use to access Web sites? How often do you use the search engines per week? Are you aware that ICT can enhance your knowledge in any area of your choice? Do you own a personal computer? Would you like to own one? Would you pay a flat fee of GH¢20–¢30 (approximately US$20–$30) per month for Internet connection? Would you want to have Internet connection at your school, work, or home? The focus was on the Internet for two reasons. First, it has a high potential for promoting technology-mediated learning and reaching out to those in the remotest parts of the world. Second, the author assumed that respondents could have a relatively high level of awareness about the Internet that could enable them to relate to the issues and provide some responses. Introducing an unfamiliar ICT application could make it impossible to obtain responses if awareness was not created. After testing the instrument, the finalized questionnaire was administered to the respondents during one of their face-to-face tutorials at their study centers. At the study centers, the male and female respondents were randomly selected for the data collection.

A thousand questionnaires were administered among 500 males and 500 females randomly selected from all ten administrative regions in Ghana. Out of the total, 656 responses, or 65.6 percent, were returned. Though samples were taken from all ten administrative regions of the country, priority was given to the most privileged and the most marginalized, in order to have a good comparison of these two contrasting areas. This was based on the assumption that availability, access to, and usage of ICT facilities would be very high in the most privileged region, which is Greater Accra—the national capital—and very low in the most marginalized part of the country, which is Northern Ghana, comprising the Upper East, Upper West, and Northern regions. As observed from the regional profile, these regions are the most deprived in terms of infrastructural and technological advancement. Poverty levels are also high in these regions. Table 1 provides the percentage of responses obtained from all the regions. All responses have been analyzed with percentages.

Demographics of Respondents

Tables 2–5 present the details of the demographics of the respondents. In terms of gender, responses were obtained from a total of 266 females and 390 males, forming a total of 40.5 percent females and almost 60 percent (59.5 percent) males. Though an equal number of females and males were sampled for the study, the return rate for males was higher than that of females. One may not want to rush to assume that women's interest in ICT is limited. In terms of age the respondents ranged from below twenty to fifty-one and above. The majority of them fell within the age range of twenty–thirty, making up 78.8 percent of the total. This gives an indication that the majority of the respondents were in their early adult stage and were mainly young professionals, and some could have been in the process of deciding on a profession. This is an age group that has a relatively higher level of curiosity about the use of ICT, for instance, and therefore would be much interested in ICT systems for education. In a survey in Korea, one of the countries that has a well-developed infrastructure, it has been observed that though the share of women researchers is only 10 percent, since 2002 the gender gap in Internet usage rate has been rapidly closing in the younger generation (six–nineteen years, twenties and thirties) (UNESCO 2003). ITU (2007) also notes that the age divide in Singapore indicates that the fifteen–twenty-nine age group does best, with a digital opportunity score of 0.80. The sixty-plus age group lags behind the national average. The total gap between young tech-savvy students and the elderly amounts to some 17 percent, with the greatest gap in rates of Internet usage.

Probably reflecting their age, a higher percentage of 78.9 were not married, and only 17.4 percent were married. The remaining were separated, divorced, or widowed. In terms of education 59.9 percent had completed secondary-level education and 30.3 percent had gone further to obtain diploma certificates. Concerning the professional backgrounds of the respondents, 5.2 percent were teachers, followed by those in the informal sector, 12 percent, then civil servants, 11.8 percent. A total of 22.7 percent were not working at all but were full-time students. Tables 17, 18, 19, and 20 give the details on the sex, age, educational, and occupational distribution of the respondents.

The study also sought to find out the number of people in a household. This was to have an idea of the number of dependents per household, which could impact the financial demands and the possibility of having excess income to invest in ICT facilities. Typical of an African household, Table 21 shows that majority of the respondents, 42.2 percent, had six–ten members in the household, followed by 36.4 percent having one–five people. Interestingly, 21.4 percent recorded a household membership of more than ten. This high level of household membership could support an ICT model that targets sharing in large households.

Table 17 Regional and Sex Distribution of Respondents

			Region										Total
			Upper West	Upper East	Northern	Brong Ahafo	Ashanti	Eastern	Western	Central	Greater Accra	Volta	
Sex	Male	Count	7	8	89	38	72	50	20	10	83	13	390
		% within Region	58.3%	50.0%	44.7%	80.9%	76.6%	58.8%	57.1%	83.3%	60.1%	72.2%	59.5%
	Female	Count	5	8	110	9	22	35	15	2	55	5	266
		% within Region	41.7%	50%	55.3%	19.1%	23.4%	41.2%	42.9%	16.7%	39.9%	27.8%	40.5%
Total		Count	12	16	199	47	94	85	35	12	138	18	656
		% within Region	100%	100%	100%	100%	100%	100%	100%	100%	100%	100%	100.0%

Source: Field Data 2008

Table 17 Regional and Sex Distribution of Respondents

Source: Field Data 2008

Table 18 Age Description of Respondents

			Age					Total
			Below 20	20-30	31-40	41-50	51 and Above	
Sex	Male	Count	36	310	40	3	1	390
		% within Age	51.4%	59.6%	67.8%	75%	50%	59.5%
	Female	Count	34	210	19	1	1	265
		% within Age	48.6%	40.4%	32.2%	25%	50%	40.5%
Total		Count	70	520	59	4	2	655
		% within Age	100%	100%	100%	100%	100%	100%

Source: Field Data 2008

Table 18 Age Description of Respondents

Source: Field Data 2008

Table 19 Educational Level

			Educational Level			Total
			SHS/GCE/O/A Level	Certificate/Diploma	Others	
Sex	Male	Count	227	124	35	386
		% within Educational Level	57.6%	62.9%	64.8%	59.8%
	Female	Count	167	73	19	259
		% within Educational Level	42.4%	37.1%	35.2%	40.2%
	Total	Count	394	197	54	645
		% within Educational Level	100%	100%	100%	100%

Source: Field Data 2008

Table 19 Educational Level Source: Field Data 2008

Table 20 Occupational Background

			Profession						Total
			Teaching	Civil Servant	Self-Employed	Others	Unemployed	Student	
Sex	Male	Count	172	39	14	50	48	50	373
		% within Profession	75.4%	49.4%	82.4%	67.6%	62.3%	32.7%	59.4%
	Female	Count	56	40	3	24	29	103	255
		% within Profession	24.6%	50.6%	17.6%	32.4%	37.7%	67.3%	40.6%
	Total	Count	228	79	17	74	77	153	628
		% within Profession	100%	100%	100%	100%	100%	100%	100%

Source: Field Data 2008

Table 20 Occupational Background Source: Field Data 2008

Table 21 Number of People in Household

			Number of People in Household			Total
			1–5	6–10	Above 10	
Sex	Male	Count	127	153	90	370
		% within Number of People in Household	56.7%	58%	68.2%	59.7%
	Female	Count	97	111	42	250
		% within Number of People in Household	43.3%	42%	31.8%	40.3%
	Total	Count	224	264	132	620
		% within Number of People in Household	100%	100%	100%	100%

Source: Field Data 2008

Table 21 Number of People in Household
Source: Field Data 2008

Knowledge of ICT and Usage

In spite of the high representation of the population from the underprivileged regions in Ghana, the overall results in Table 22 reveal that 84 percent of the respondents knew what ICT was. Only 16 percent responded "no." Similarly, 90.5 percent responded that ICT could be used to enhance their knowledge in any area of choice. Only 8.9 percent didn't know. This shows that there is a high level of knowledge of ICT among the respondents, which is a good indicator for exploring the potential of ICT for development and education, most especially among the underprivileged in the third world.

The gender breakdown of the responses provides some variations. Out of the 84 percent who knew what ICT was,

63 percent were males and 37 percent were females (Table 22). From Table 23, 66.6 percent of the males indicated that they use the Internet, and 52.7 percent of the females and 47.3 percent of the males indicated that they don't use the Internet. As to where they access the Internet, Table 24 shows that 66 percent of the males and 33.3 percent of the females indicated home, 50 percent of both sexes indicated their office, and 65.6 percent of the males and 31.4 percent of the females checked Internet café. It is exciting to note that an equal percentage of both males and females access the Internet from the office, compared with the variations in percentages in the use of Internet cafés and home. This implies that women in the formal sector who could be assumed to have relatively higher educational qualifications access the Internet on equal terms with their male colleagues. Probably because of the burden of their domestic responsibilities, the majority of women are not able to go beyond their immediate environs of accessibility, which in this case is their office, to use the Internet in cafés and even their homes. This gives an indication that if Internet services were provided for women in a convenient environment where they could also have some leisure, such as the workplace, they would equal their male counterparts in the usage of the Internet. This confirms the argument from research on women and technology that facilities have to be sited at places that suit women (UNESCO 2003).

Table 22 Knowledge of ICT

			Do you know what ICT is?		Total
			Yes	No	
Sex	Male	Count	342	46	388
		% within Do you know what ICT is?	63%	43.4%	59.8%
	Female	Count	201	60	261
		% within Do you know what ICT is?	37%	56.6%	40.2%
	Total	Count	543	106	649
		% within Do you know what ICT is?	100%	100%	100%

Source: Field Data 2008

Table 22 Knowledge of ICT Source: Field Data 2008

Table 23 Usage of the Internet

			Do you use the Internet?		Total
			Yes	No	
Sex	Male	Count	275	115	390
		% within Do you use the Internet?	66.6%	47.3%	59.5%
	Female	Count	138	128	266
		% within Do you use the Internet?	33.4%	52.7%	40.5%
Total		Count	413	243	656
		% within Do you use the Internet?	100%	100%	100%

Source: Field Data 2008

Table 23 Usage of the Internet Source: Field Data 2008

Table 24 Where Respondents Access the Internet

			If yes, where do you access the Internet?				Total
			Home	Office	Internet Café	All of the Above	
Sex	Male	Count	8	20	229	17	274
		% within If yes, where do you access the Internet?	66.7%	50%	68.6%	63%	66.3%
	Female	Count	4	20	105	10	139
		% within If yes, where do you access the Internet?	33.3%	50%	31.4%	37%	33.7%
Total		Count	12	40	334	27	413
		% within If yes, where do you access the Internet?	100%	100%	100%	100%	100%

Source: Field Data 2008

Table 24 Where Respondents Access the Internet Source: Field Data 2008

There were gender variations in relation to duration of browsing as well. In finding out how long respondents stayed on the Internet, the number of men increased in percentage as the time increased, whereas the number of women decreased in percentage. Interestingly, the same percentage of males and females—57 percent—were able to browse up to thirty minutes. Table 25 shows that 73.5 percent of males browsed from thirty-one to fifty-nine minutes, and 26.5 percent of females did. For those who browsed between an hour and an hour and a half, males formed 73.5 percent and females formed 28.5 percent. For those able to browse more than two hours 74.3 percent were males, whereas 25.7 percent were females. So the majority of the women were able to browse up to thirty minutes, which equals the amount of their male colleagues. Apart from that, the female percentage decreased as the duration increased, whereas the male percentage increased as the duration increased. Is it the issue of lack of time for women to go online, inability to use the cafés after work, or because they don't have the space and time at home and therefore as a result of domestic responsibilities don't even look for the opportunity to browse at home or after work? Probably beyond the workplace most women don't browse the Internet. This presents an opportunity for promoting workplace browsing for women, though this could have limitations, depending on the demands of work and its regulations. Women may also have to be encouraged to look for time outside their office work to use the Internet.

The times of browsing per week somehow followed the duration trend. Whereas 65.5 percent of males browsed once a week, only 34.5 percent of the females did so; 67.4 percent of the males versus 32.4 percent of the females browsed three times a week. A total of 78.3 percent of the males and 21.7 percent of the females browsed occasionally. Table 26 shows that a higher percentage of the males browsed on a regular basis, but the story is different for females. More males were regular users of the Internet than females.

Table 25 Duration of Stay on the Internet

			If yes, how long on average do you stay on the Internet?					Total
			Up to 30 mins	31-59 mins	1 hr-1 hr 30 mins	1hr 31 mins-2 hrs	More than 2 hrs	
Sex	Male	Count	54	50	108	36	26	274
		If yes, how long on average do you stay on the Internet?	50%	73.5%	71.5%	72%	74.3%	66.5%
	Female	Count	54	18	43	14	9	138
		If yes, how long on average do you stay on the Internet?	50%	26.5%	28.5%	28%	25.7%	33.5%
Total		Count	108	68	151	50	35	412
		If yes, how long on average do you stay on the Internet?	100%	100%	100%	100%	100%	100%

Source: Field Data 2008

Table 25 Duration of Stay on the Internet

Source: Field Data 2008

Table 26 Times per Week that use the Café

			If yes, how many times per week do you use the café?					Total
			Once	Twice	Three Times	More than Three Times	Occasional	
Sex	Male	Count	91	71	48	31	18	259
		If yes, how many times per week do you use the café?	65.5%	66.4%	67.6%	67.4%	78.3%	67.1%
	Female	Count	48	36	23	15	5	127
		If yes, how many times per week do you use the café?	34.5%	33.6%	32.4%	32.6%	21.7%	32.9%
Total		Count	139	107	71	46	23	386
		If yes, how many times per week do you use the café?	100%	100%	100%	100%	100%	100%

Source: Field Data 2008

Table 26 Times per Week to Use the Café
Source: Field Data 2008

Payment for Internet services also varied across gender. Following the poverty patterns, the results revealed that more men pay higher fees than women. A total of 64.8 percent of the males and 35.2 percent of the females paid fifty pesewa per hour, and 62.5 percent of the males and 37.5 percent of the females paid one cedi an hour. Again 60 percent of the males and 40 percent of the females paid a cedi and twenty pesewa an hour. The percentage of men was steadily high as the fee increased from half a cedi.

Concerning usage, Table 27 shows that 57.5 percent of the males and 42.5 percent of the females used the Internet to send e-mail, and 51.3 percent of the males and 48.7 percent of the females used the Internet to chat with friends. From Table 28, 69.8 percent of the males and 30.2 percent of the females indicated that they were aware of search engines such as Google. The results in Table 29 on frequency of usage of search engines indicate that 67.2 percent of the males and 32.8 percent of the females used the search engines once a week; 71 percent of the males and 29 percent of the females used it more than three times a week. Table 30 presents the results on the question of whether they use the search engines to access educational materials. From the results 68.4 percent of the males and 31.6

percent of the females indicated that they use the search engines to access educational materials. Results in Table 31 also show that 61.5 percent of the males and 38.6 percent of the females indicated that they are aware that ICT could be used to enhance their knowledge in any area of their choice.

Table 27 What Respondents use the Internet for

			What do you use the Internet for?				Total
			Send E-mail Only	Chat with Friends	Other	All of the Above	
Sex	Male	Count	69	20	76	99	264
		What do you use the Internet for?	57.5%	51.3%	73.8%	72.8%	66.3%
	Female	Count	51	19	27	37	134
		What do you use the Internet for?	42.5%	48.7%	26.2%	27.2%	33.7%
Total		Count	120	39	103	136	398
		What do you use the Internet for?	100%	100%	100%	100%	100%

Source: Field Data 2008

Table 27 What Respondents Use the Internet For
Source: Field Data 2008

Table 28 Awareness of the Use of the Search Engines to Access Web Sites

			Are you aware of search engines such as Google that you can use to access Web sites?		Total
			Yes	No	
Sex	Male	Count	254	101	355
		Are you aware of search engines such as Google that you can use to access Web sites?	69.8%	43.3%	59.5%
	Female	Count	110	132	242
		Are you aware of search engines such as Google that you can use to access Web sites?	30.2%	56.7%	40.5%
Total		Count	364	233	597
		Are you aware of search engines such as Google that you can use to access Web sites?	100%	100%	100%

Source: Field Data 2008

Table 28 Awareness of the Use of the Search Engines to Access Web Sites Source: Field Data 2008

Table 29 How Often Respondents Access the Search Engines per Week

			If yes, how often do you use the search engines per week?					Total
			Once	Twice	Three Times	Over Three Times	Occasional	
Sex	Male	Count	92	59	27	49	8	235
		If yes, how often do you use the search engines per week?	67.2%	71.1%	64.3%	71%	66.7%	68.5%
	Female	Count	45	24	15	20	4	108
		If yes, how often do you use the search engines per week?	32.8%	28.9%	35.7%	29%	33.3%	31.5%
Total		Count	137	83	42	69	12	343
		If yes, how often do you use the search engines per week?	100%	100%	100%	100%	100%	100%

Source: Field Data 2008

Table 29 How Often Respondents Access the Search Engines per Week Source: Field Data 2008

Table 30 Use of Search Engines to Access Educational Materials

			If yes, do you use search engines to access educational materials?		Total
			Yes	No	
Sex	Male	Count	201	38	239
		If yes, do you use search engines to access educational materials?	68.4%	69.1%	68.5%
	Female	Count	93	17	110
		If yes, do you use search engines to access educational materials?	31.6%	30.9%	31.5%
Total		Count	294	55	349
		If yes, do you use search engines to access educational materials?	100%	100%	100%

Source: Field Data 2008

Table 30 Use of Search Engines to Access Educational Materials Source: Field Data 2008

Table 31 Awareness of Use of ICT to Enhance Knowledge

			Are you aware that ICT can enhance your knowledge in any area of your choice?		Total
			Yes	No	
Sex	Male	Count	343	25	368
		Are you aware that ICT can enhance your knowledge in any area of your choice?	61.5%	42.4%	59.6%
	Female	Count	215	34	249
		Are you aware that ICT can enhance your knowledge in any area of your choice?	38.5%	57.6%	40.4%
Total		Count	558	59	617
		Are you aware that ICT can enhance your knowledge in any area of your choice?	100%	100%	100%

Source: Field Data 2008

Table 31 Awareness of Use of ICT to Enhance Knowledge

Source: Field Data 2008

Ownership of Personal Computers and Desire for Connectivity

Gender differentials of results on ownership of personal computers were similar to the initial observations. Table 32 shows that 71.6 percent of the males and 28.4 percent of the females said they owned personal computers. Those who did not own them were asked whether they would like to, and according to the results in Table 33, 55.1 percent of the males and 44.9 percent of the females said yes. As indicated in Table 34, 59.5 percent of the males and 40.5 percent of the females said they would like to have Internet connection at their school, work, or home. In Table 35, 61.2 percent of the males and 38.8 percent of the females said they would like to pay a flat fee of a cedi equivalent of US$20–$30 per month for Internet connection.

Table 32 Ownership of Personal Computer

			Do you own a personal computer?		Total
			Yes	No	
Sex	Male	Count	136	244	380
		Do you own a personal computer?	71.6%	54.6%	59.7%
	Female	Count	54	203	257
		Do you own a personal computer?	28.4%	45.4%	40.3%
Total		Count	190	447	637
		% within Do you own a personal computer?	100%	100%	100%

Source: Field Data 2008

Table 32 Ownership of Personal Computer
Source: Field Data 2008

Table 33 Desire to Own Personal Computer

			If no, would you like to own one?		Total
			Yes	No	
Sex	Male	Count	243	4	247
		If no, would you like to own one?	55.1%	36.4%	54.6%
	Female	Count	198	7	205
		If no, would you like to own one?	44.9%	63.6%	45.4%
Total		Count	441	11	452
		If no, would you like to own one?	100%	100%	100.%

Source: Field Data 2008

Table 33 Desire to Own Personal Computer
Source: Field Data 2008

Table 34 Desire to Have Internet Connection at Your School, at Work, or at Home

			Would you want to have Internet connection at your school, work, or home?		Total
			Yes	No	
Sex	Male	Count	355	20	375
		Would you want to have Internet connection at your school, work, or home?	59.5%	60.6%	59.5%
	Female	Count	242	13	255
		Would you want to have Internet connection at your school, work, or home?	40.5%	39.4%	40.5%
Total		Count	597	33	630
		Would you want to have Internet connection at your school, work, or home?	100%	100%	100%

Source: Field Data 2008

Table 34 Desire to Have Internet Connection at Your School, at Work, or at Home Source: Field Data 2008

Table 35 Willingness to Pay a Flat Fee of GH¢20–¢30 per Month for Internet Connection

			If yes, would you pay a flat fee of GH¢20–¢30 per month for Internet connection?		Total
			Yes	No	
Sex	Male	Count	241	123	364
		If yes, would you pay a flat fee of GH¢20–¢30 per month for Internet connection?	61.2%	56.4%	59.5%
	Female	Count	153	95	248
		If yes, would you pay a flat fee of GH¢20–¢30 per month for Internet connection?	38.8%	43.6%	40.5%
Total		Count	394	218	612
		If yes, would you pay a flat fee of GH¢20–¢30 per month for Internet connection?	100%	100%	100%

Source: Field Data 2008

Table 35 Willingness to Pay a Flat Fee of GH¢20–¢30 per Month for Internet Connection Source: Field Data 2008

Generally the results reveal that men had higher percentage responses to almost all the issues raised such as knowledge and usage of Internet, duration and rate of usage of Internet facilities, access to the Internet, payment of fees for service charges, ownership of personal computers, and desire for connectivity. As expressed in most of the literature on women and ICT use, compared with their male counterparts women are at a disadvantaged position. However, one may take consolation from the fact that a percentage of women have a growing interest in accessing and using ICT facilities. Most interestingly, despite the estimated high levels of poverty among women, 40 percent of females versus 60 percent of males are willing to pay a cedi equivalent of US$1.20 for an hour's use of the Internet. This is encouraging enough.

The workplace has also been found to be a convenient place for working women to use the Internet. This brings to light the issue of space and women's usage of Internet facilities. It could be that in addition to the time demanding nature of domestic responsibilities, the issue of women not having the right to share certain public places with men is a factor in women's limited usage of cafés. Or could it also be that because of the relatively high poverty levels and the competing demands for their limited resources, the women were constrained by money to use existing Internet cafés or own personal computers and connectivity in the homes? If conscious gender-specific efforts are made, there is no doubt that both women and men could have some level of access and utilize ICT facilities in their studies at a distance.

This chapter has looked at a survey among distance learners in Ghana. From the regional profile one could see that there isn't much advancement in the provision of Internet facilities, for instance, across the regions of the country. Only the Greater Accra Region and a few others such as the Western Region have made modest improvement in ICT infrastructural development as indicated by the availability of Internet services and mobile telephony. The study of the distance learners has, however, revealed that in their private day-to-day life most of the students know ICT (84 percent) and use it for basic activities such as Internet browsing, e-mail, and chatting with friends. More than 90 percent indicated that ICT could be used to enhance their knowledge in any area of choice. In spite of the gender variations the results from both sexes could be used to inform policy direction on the use of ICT to support education at a distance. ICT resources could be a good support system for distance learners to overcome the challenge of information flow and minimal interaction. The results give some indication of the possibility of using the country's limited available ICT resources for educational purposes that will meet the basic educational needs of the students who are engaged in distance learning.

Chapter 9

Women and ODL

Using the case of the United States it is noted in a recent government document that, the average distance learning student is 34 years old, employed part-time, has previous college credit—and is a woman (U.S. Senate in Kramarae 2001).

The demands and pressure of society, work, and family have put pressure on women to pursue further studies not only for enrichment purposes but also to meet all of life's aspirations. Meanwhile the same pressures that push women to pursue further studies usually make it impossible for them to take their courses on campus. To be able to meet all their societal, home, and family responsibilities women opt for open and distance learning programs (ODL). A report by the American Association of University Women (AAUW) Educational Foundation has found that distance or online learning is on the rise and that women make up the majority of students. Sixty percent of these nontraditional online learners are over twenty-five years of age and female (Kramarae 2001). The distance learning arrangement, however, does not entirely release them of their burden but rather adds up to their already heavy "excess baggage." Meanwhile this is "excess baggage" that they cannot choose to drop, but is a load they must carry if they seek to succeed in almost all aspects of life.

The use of information and communication technology (ICT) in distance education no doubt offers new opportunities for women to achieve their educational goals. Meanwhile AAUW has noted that working mothers interested in furthering their education are doing so online and adding a difficult "third shift" to their responsibilities as mothers and employees. This chapter looks at the potential of ODL for creating educational opportunities for women, and the challenges therein.

The ODL Potential for Women's Lifestyles

By its nature of being a type of teaching and learning that can be offered from anywhere and be accessed from anywhere by anybody at any time and in any way, open and distance learning has been able to respond to the educational needs of women in particular (Mhehe 2006; Olakunein and Ojo 2006; Moffat 1997). Several scholars have assessed this potential of ODL for women. Prümmer (2000) observes in her book *Women and Distance Education: Challenges and Opportunities* and other writings that a wide variety of evidence from different countries supports the conclusion that open and distance learning has the potential to provide equal opportunities in higher and continuing education. She notes further that distance education, although involving a degree of risk to the stability of families and relationships, among others, nevertheless offers women a chance that, on balance, is worth taking. One of the best ways to educate women is by ODL. ODL provides opportunities that enhance the educational qualifications of women and raise their occupational bargaining power (Demiray and Curabay 2000).

Most women who desire to pursue further studies are faced with hindrances that do not apply to men so much. Most women have to find a way of combining job, community work, family responsibilities, and academic work if they decide to go to school. In this process some of the women who take on-campus courses become faced with inflexible class schedules, inadequate child care, and financial difficulties, among others. ODL thus provides excellent opportunities for women who have children, heavy work responsibilities, disabilities, or tight schedules, or who reside in geographically isolated areas. And for those women who are desperate to have a flexible learning plan, ODL thus becomes a dream come true. ODL overcomes most of the divides that women face—be it along professional lines, religious borders, or in the domestic housekeeping and socio-cultural arena. Olakuein and Ojo (2006) have indicated that the uniqueness of ODL as a women empowerment strategy can be gleaned from the fact that it straddles so many facets of the social system.

Faith and Sturrock (1990) note that the clear advantage of ODL is that students can study in their own home on their own time. Given that women are more likely than men to interrupt their education and careers for parenthood and temporary confinement to the home, the advantages of distance education for women are obvious. The authors note further that advantages extend beyond the needs of women confined to the home or those isolated in remote places; a wide variety of women in every province have found ODL—in other words, independent home study—an attractive option.

On the religious front, a survey report by Rawaf, Haya Saad Al, Simmons, and Cyril (1992) reveals strong support for an open university for women in Saudi Arabia. The authors note that such an institution would greatly increase access for women to higher education and at the same time be compatible with Islamic custom concerning the segregation of the sexes and a woman's primary role as wife and mother.

Across professions, Pym (1992) gives a report on the rapid growth of ODL programs for nurses. The author explains that ODL tends to mean different things in different institutions, ranging from the "industrial model" self-study course package with limited teacher-student interaction to the fully interactive audio- and videoconferencing of the "virtual classroom" for all professionals, including nurses.

When it is about education, time may be a more precious commodity than money for most women. ODL gives women the ability to control their time and coordinate work, school, and home responsibilities. On the issue of flexibility Kramarae (2001) notes in her study that a community college program director who has taken both types of classes preferred distance learning because it "allowed me to work on classwork on my schedule. ... I could take my laptop on business trips and work on classwork in hotels or work early morning hours or on the weekend. [I was] not locked into a specific class time/place." Thus some women appreciate the flexibility of the online learning process itself and the ability to study at their own pace without schedule restrictions.

Distance education has also helped some women minimize child care costs and also travel cost to the campus in case they were to take on-campus courses. The response of a thirty-one-year-old salesclerk and part-time student indicates a typical picture that "I really prefer to learn through discussions, but right now we need to save money, and I need to stay home with my children. My husband would be in favor of distance education since I would be able to care for my children instead of putting them in day care" (Kramarae 2001).

ODL also meet special needs of some women. Working online often alleviates problems of access associated with physical disabilities. Some of the women in Karamae's study define *handicap* to include lack of transportation, child care, or even a handicap on the part of an institution with a limited number of faculty, courses, and programs that are all addressed in ODL programs. Some older women also opt for ODL courses because they feel out of place in the younger environment of a traditional classroom.

Facilitating Factors and Categories of Women in ODL Programs

ODL has been found to be advantageous for all categories of women. The factors that drive women to pursue ODL courses are similar but different when comparing the developed and the developing communities. The study by Olakuein and Ojo (2006) in the Nigerian context and research by the AAUW Educational Foundation by Kramarae (2001) set in the United States will be discussed to assess the factors that push women to pursue further studies at a distance.

Based on the Nigerian context, Olakuein and Ojo (2006) have provided four categories of women who could find distance education an opportunity for meeting their life aspirations. One category of women is those who are full-time housewives by their own choice or that of their husbands, with the objective of taking full care of their children and husbands. As a result they may not be able to leave home, children, and husband to settle on campus for further studies. Some of these women may have dropped out of formal education at an early age or completed just basic or secondary education. Women in this category may want to upgrade their knowledge and skills to become better homemakers, look for new jobs when their children have grown, or obtain a degree to serve as a role model for their children, ODL becomes a good option for them. For such women ODL could be a means of fulfilling their life dreams of raising a good family and upgrading themselves at the same time.

A second category of women is those who cannot access education as a result of religious or cultural practices of segregation. As a result of their obedience and commitment to religious and cultural practices they might not have tasted formal education at all. For some such women who in their later years desire to benefit from formal education, ODL provides an alternative arrangement and an opportunity. Again there are cultural and religious reformations going on all over at a very fast rate, so some societies are changing and making flexible regulations for its members. The adult women in such societies may want to take advantage of an ODL program to educate themselves.

The other class of women discussed in the Nigerian context by Olakuein and Ojo (2006) is the itinerant nomadic women whose vocational practices require that they move regularly with their families. Formal education in these societies is not a priority. For generation after generation, women in these societies have been denied access to quality education of whatever form because of the peripatetic nature of their livelihood. Women of such societies could benefit from the ODL model if they are made aware of the essence of formal education for their subsistence lifestyle and that of their families. An ODL approach that will not physically eliminate them from their social environments and still assure them of quality education could appeal to such people.

The fourth category of women is the working wives and mothers who have a strong desire to raise a good family and make it to the top in their career as well. These two top visions demand time and financial resources to accomplish. Most such women have had formal education up to a certain level but need to study further. Some may require first degrees, master's degrees, PhD degrees, or professional upgradement certificates. Meanwhile, leaving home and children, and in some instances the job, to go back to school becomes just impossible. This is where ODL provides a better option for them, so that they can keep all their responsibilities and study at the same time. This could be very challenging for such women. They have to manage all the *three shifts* with much stress and energy.

Kamarae (2001) also discusses various perceptions of American women and the reasons for which they pursue educational programs at a distance, which in their case is online. The women on ODL programs have been found to include degree seekers, pragmatists, those who study for study's sake (whom the author called lifelong learners), the poor, the career changers, and the disappointed.

- Degree seekers are the women who value the credential, personal enrichment, and knowledge they acquire through online classes. Such women seek an associate degree as an intermediate step in a longer process of educational and occupational preparation. They aspire to complete the entire degree program online, probably in view of its convenience for them. For some of the respondents, ODL will be part of their life. The authors quote one of the respondents as follows: "I am already earning my bachelor's online and will try to do my master's the same way."
- The pragmatists include those who take online classes so that they will advance or develop their careers. A forty-nine-year-old alumni director is quoted as saying, "I am using distance education right now to obtain a degree for career advancement. I don't think I could ever call this pleasure."
- The lifelong learners cover the category of women who might have obtained several degrees but still want to take online courses for the pleasure of understanding and knowledge.
- The interested poor unfortunately are those women who are interested in online education but too poor to access it. According to the author, some of the women indicated that distance learning could solve time constraints but not financial constraints.
- The career changers make up the category of women whose desire for online learning is for the purpose of making their lives better. Their goal is to use distance learning to change career paths to meet their monetary needs but not emotional needs.

- The disappointed interestingly include those who desire to pursue a degree program at a distance but cannot find the type of program they want online.

These illustrations help give us a good idea of the different categories of women who need ODL programs to leapfrog. Having different target groups of women implies that ODL programs should be packaged in such a way that they meet the needs of all the different categories of women. With the flexibility and innovation that ODL presents, this should not be an impossible venture. One critical target group of the women is those who are disappointed because the type of course they want is not offered. This is worth considering if ODL is to be used to provide equitable access to education. Much as it has budgetary implications, conscious effort has to be made to offer a wide range of courses that students can choose from (Crag 1991; Effeh 1991; Demiray and Curabay 2000; Fontaine 2002).

Challenges Women Face in ODL Programs

European Context

It is interesting to note that the very factors that push women to opt for ODL courses—or in other words the barriers that ODL seeks to overcome—tend to be the challenges that they face in the ODL programs. May (1994) noted from the stories of the women in her study that the experience of studying via distance was significantly different for female learners than for male learners. Although they praised distance study, the women interviewees unanimously agreed that ODL *isn't for everyone*. Distance learning was found to be easier for men than women. For the women, family responsibilities remained the same as they took on the role of student. Because distance study requires a considerable degree of learner self-determination and self-motivation, the women contended that it was best suited to self-starters. Women who withdrew from courses did so for reasons they identified as relating to their lack of self-discipline. The author therefore concluded that ODL as a study mode can be an important educational alternative for women, but does not represent a panacea for all the problems of access to traditional educational systems (May 1994).

In a similar vein Kramarae (2001) writes about "the third shift." By *third shift* the author means that ODL often adds another layer to a woman's workday; women have to find time for a "third shift" of study time and online classes early in the morning or late at night, in the free time between the first shift of a full-time job and the second shift of homemaking or taking care of children. This way women who take ODL courses face substantially more challenges than their male counterparts.

Again, ODL courses could be just as expensive as conventional school programs because, as some authors put it, they may include some hidden costs, such as expensive technology and subscriptions to online services, though this may depend on the mode of delivery and other factors. Phillip (1993) has noted that the main difficulties hindering women from continuing their studies seem to be the interrelated problems of financial sponsorship and pressure from family and society not to continue education. Moffatt (1997) indicates that financial, attitudinal, and skills barriers may need to be overcome by women in ODL programs.

In a study by Spronk (1990) in Europe the author found that women have more transportation problems than men. In both countries that were studied, women have more restricted access to a car as an independent means of transport and must rely more on others or on public transport to get to a study center. In the study, eight out of ten men said that they either own a car or have unrestricted access to one. By contrast, only six in ten women in one institution and seven in ten women in another institution had their own cars or could get one whenever they needed it.

A major obstacle to attendance is the pressure of family and personal commitments such as taking care of children or a relative, the arrival of a new baby, moving into a new house, and children's involvement in sports. Women are affected much more by all these commitments, except maybe the last. Family commitments are not only time-consuming but also lead to a loss of flexibility. Women may therefore find it extremely difficult to fit visits to a study center into their schedules. For most women it is the overwhelming problem of juggling their studies in addition to work and family commitments that makes it difficult to attend the study center. Some women may also find it difficult to attend tutorials because their partners may not be available to provide child care or transportation.

This is where Internet-based or electronic-oriented support systems become very useful for such women. In this case they will not be required to make regular travels to study centers for tutorials or examinations. Much as European institutions might have advanced from this kind of practice, this is what is currently being done in some African countries, and Ghana has to fully get on board (Evans 1995; Faith and Sturrock 1990; Faith 1988; Grace 1994; Hipp 1997; Kanwar 1990; Jeffries 1999; Kirkup and Prummer 1990). The question is this: how could we explore the potential of ICT to address all such barriers?

African Context

A study by Olakuein and Ojo (2006) that was done in East Africa also revealed some gender issues in ODL that are similar to the challenges that European women face. Based on stories about everyday realities of the female students, the authors noted that many had had to overcome time constraints, cultural expectations, and financial obstacles regarding their higher education. On the issue of time constraints the students complained that they were tired all the time because of too much work. One student was quoted to have remarked, "If I try to study, I feel sleepy. If I force myself to study, I find myself reading with very little understanding because the brain and the body are tired. They need some rest, but I cannot rest because at 5:30 in the morning I am required to be up again to prepare for the family breakfast and go to a full day's work." As a strategy a fourth-year student who might have gained experience over the years indicated that since she enrolled in the program, she was compelled to study in the brief periods between her chores and other demands in her life. This obviously made her tired and was a contributing factor to her poor academic performance. She expressed that in addition to her tight family and work schedules, she had to be away approximately eighty-five days per year to attend compulsory study activities at the regional center. While away from her family and employment, she had to pay for transportation, food, accommodation, and health care.

With this kind of stress on the students it is not surprising for the author to find that when they were asked about the possible use of alternative learning technologies, one woman suggested that her most pressing need was not for learning technologies, but for other technologies such as a washing machine, stove and a vacuum cleaner, which could help shorten the time she spent on housework and increase the time she needed for studying.

There is also an African problem of study materials not being ready at the time students need them. Many women have told similar stories about the difficulties of obtaining study materials on time and not having enough time at home to study. They saw these problems as barriers that discouraged many women from even enrolling in the ODL programs. Some explained that a major reason why most enrolled women abandoned their studies was their inability to meet the logistical demands placed on them by the school's system.

The East African study, specifically Tanzania, emphasizes that in many situations, the woman not only runs the household, holds a full-time job, and looks after the children, but is also responsible for small farming projects such as raising chickens or cows or tilling gardens and fields to augment her income.

There are some more cultural expectations that affect female distance learners in the African context. The position of the husband is pivotal. And if the husbands would allow their wives freedom to make decisions for their own lives and act on them, many women would be studying at a distance by combining their multiple roles in whatever circumstances are possible in their families. In one case a schoolteacher registered and paid about 60 percent of her fees but had to drop out because her husband refused to give her permission, with the reason that she had many other family responsibilities, and if she started the program, there would be nobody to take care of the family. The husband expressed the fear that she would concentrate on the course and not have time to think about family matters. In another instance a primary schoolteacher who was married with five children complained that her efforts to be a student had been stifled after only six months of struggle because her husband prevented her from doing anything on weekends other than take care of family responsibilities: the children, the cows, the farm, receiving visitors, and visiting. The husband is quoted to have remarked that "Ah, ah, school work! This you can do other days when I am not home. When I am home, I do not like you to do that." On evenings that she could study, the husband would turn off the lights, claiming that the electricity bills were too high and demanding that she study in the daytime. There were also instances of men picking up their wives' study materials and not allowing them to study. The traditional cultures and some religious practices in Africa where men (husbands, fathers, brothers, grandfathers, or uncles) control female relatives in all aspects of their lives can affect women negatively. Women (wives, mothers, sisters, grandmothers, or aunts) most often do not have the power to take action or make final decisions that might improve their lives or those of others, including other women or children in their families.

A similar observation has been made by Cragg, Andrusyszyn, and Fraser (2005) that although it is likely that most men, as well as women, are supportive of their spouse's educational aspirations, several female adult students reported in their study that their mates had refused to accommodate their need for quiet study time. There were reports of extreme cases where women's husbands had hidden or damaged their study materials and assignments in efforts to sabotage their educational ambitions.

Through culture and socialization, most women are taught that husbands and other men are not to participate in any tasks or roles that are traditionally ascribed to women. Many women thus unquestioningly carry out all the unpaid family work, their paid work in employment, and other life tasks such as studying. Without their husbands' permission and support they cannot use their own money to even enroll in the program. Some women even have restrictions in interacting with male course-mates. Most of the female students also have financial difficulties because they are obligated to use their income to support family members.

It is not surprising that the author found that most of the female students were widows, single parents, Catholic sisters, unmarried women in their late thirties and early forties, and women whose husbands had retired. Maybe these were the ones who were not under any or as much male control and could therefore have the freedom to pursue their interests.

Apart from home care, male control, and socio-cultural intimidations, career is another factor that makes many demands on African career women, especially when they choose to study at a distance, which is often without having study leave. Most career women take ODL courses in professional and other programs to achieve credentials or maintain competence. In an interview by Cragg, Andrusyszyn, and Fraser (2005) of women in nursing, health studies, and accounting programs respondents indicated that they managed a mean of six roles in addition to being students. Women in professions face particular pressure because of expectations from professional organizations, licensing bodies, and the public that they should be able to maintain professional competence throughout their careers. One way of accomplishing this is by engaging in continuous education or lifelong learning. It is assumed that taking advantage of educational opportunities at a distance enables them to easily meet their work and family obligations, but these flexible learning opportunities rather turn out to give them a *third shift*. These multiple roles affect their well-being (Dunlop 2004ab; Creed, Allsop, Mills, and Morpheth 2005).

Instructional materials for ODL are designed to be self-explanatory and usable for independent learning. But Rathore, Singh, Kumar, and Dubey (1996) have refuted the idea that instructional materials adequately serve the purposes and induce self-learning in women students. Maybe as a result of the stress from their multiple roles, women at times have difficulty understanding the content. Instructional materials may not always be all that explanatory for the women especially when they have to study it with some tiredness and stress. Because of the personal and social engagements and responsibilities women may get less time to devote themselves fully and freely to learning materials. As a result women usually have a strong desire for tutorial support as needed.

The Way Out

ODL programs have been found to be convenient for women to pursue further studies, but in the process they are faced with many more challenges. There should be a way to help them out in this situation so that they can make the best of ODL for their professional advancement. This is where special support systems for women become critical. Women could be supported from different sources, including the use of the very factors that give them challenges such as the home (spouse and children), extended family, friends, place of work, study-mates, and the ODL institutions. The use of ICT is one remarkable way of supporting the women as well.

Spousal Support

The biggest challenge most women have faced in their study programs is the disapproval of their spouses. Without their husbands' permission some women cannot even use their own money to enroll in a program. Some women have been successful in ODL programs because they have had the full support of their spouses. In the study by Cragg, Andrusyszyn, and Fraser (2005) spouses were rated as the most important support in the home context, as well as the most supportive group for the women. Some spouses took on additional roles. The women worked things out with the partner to ensure that household tasks were done, that children were cared for, and that some limited amount of social life was preserved, all of which required negotiation with the spouse. One woman commented, "While I'm taking a course, my husband has to take over the laundry, cooking and cleaning that I normally do in addition to the vacuuming, household maintenance and cleaning he usually does. I could not do this course without his support." The most excited ones were those whose spouses were proud of them for pursuing ODL courses. For some women even though their spouses were impatient for them to complete their programs, at least they had their support and had helped them to reapportion work. Some of these supportive spouses took consolation in the fact that the wife could learn at home instead of traveling, which helped to preserve the family unit.

Children's Support

Child care is another big hurdle for women/mothers in their academic programs. Because in some cultures women have the sole responsibility for managing the children and the home, it puts the burden on the women. It is child care that makes most women opt for ODL programs, but it turns out to be the biggest challenge for them. That is why for some women, their only option is to wait till their children have grown to an independent stage; then they can pursue further studies, whether at a distance or on campus.

There are some possible solutions, however. Toddlers may be very difficult to handle, but when they are given some orientation, they may calm down and focus on their games and studies when Mummy is studying. Teens could also be very supportive and willing to take up any chore in the house to help if told that *Mummy has to study*. Some will contribute by not making unnecessary demands on their mothers. Some children become proud of their mothers going to school and therefore offer to help them even with their housework. One respondent in a study by Cragg, Andrusyszyn, and Fraser (2005) said, "My son and I have often spent time at the dining room table doing our homework together. I think it has had a positive effect on his outlook towards school and the fact that learning does not end with grade 12."

Extended Family and Communal Support

The extended family and the entire community could protest a woman's/mother's "going to school" on grounds that "the woman's place is the kitchen." Meanwhile with the changing trends in society and the sensitization from women's empowerment interventions the extended family and the community at large could be a great support to the education of women.

The support of the extended family and the entire community cannot be underestimated for women who choose to study, especially in African communities where there is strong communal bond. In Africa mothers, fathers, siblings, grandparents, aunts, uncles, cousins, nieces, nephews, neighbors, and friends all care about each other and are willing to offer any service that they are capable of. It is not culturally acceptable for one to say no when the request is within the person's capacity. In such contexts, members of the extended family and the community can and do offer to help the student with child care, home care, laundry, and all other services that the person will require. Some even offer to let a younger member stay with the student mother to help her. It is unfortunate that these social systems are gradually breaking down in the African context because of the influence of the Western culture. It is also prudent for women who get support from any of these sources to adequately reward such people. They should not abuse or take undue advantage of such systems.

Workplace Support

Paid work is another area that poses a great challenge to women when they opt to pursue further studies at a distance. Study leave is not normally offered in such learning arrangements, so students have to combine work and study. It could be manageable in some instances if the women had to combine work with only studies, as most men have always managed to do. But it is a critical combination for women because of the excess load of home keeping and child care. Married male colleagues in the workplace are assured of having their wives handle all the domestic aspects of their life. Some men have the privilege of having their wives not only cook for them, clean the house, and take care of the children, but also wash and iron their clothes for them or supervise someone who does it. What a relief. Such men must be grateful to these women.

This is what society has denied most women unless they *buy* it for themselves by hiring the services of someone.

As a result women find it tough to live up to standard at the workplace the moment they take up the extra responsibility of studying further. Most bosses (heads of organizations), who are mostly men and therefore have their domestic or family life taken care of by their wives, cannot comprehend the plight of their female staff and give them any relief or support. Some such bosses rather require much from their female staff. Similarly some male colleagues may not be willing to cover for their female colleagues.

It will be much easier when a female worker is able to gain the support of her supervisor, colleagues, and subordinates so that her work can be managed in such a way that she can confidently pursue her triple roles.

Some women, however, have benefited much from workplace support. Some employers could support their employees with time off for study, especially during examination periods, financial reimbursement to support tuition fees, and recognition of their certificates for promotion. It is unfortunate that some employees meet opposition and roadblocks from colleagues and immediate supervisors. Most often it depends on the kind of relationship they have with colleagues and their willingness to support them when they need help. Women who benefit from the workplace support need to be appreciative.

Use of Hiring Services and Household Equipment

Tied to the support from the workplace are the financial resources that can enable women to invest in hiring services and the purchase of household equipment. As society changes, different support services are popping up for working and studying mothers. Probably in recognition of the stress of combining the triple roles, organizations are being set up to offer laundry, housecleaning, catering, and child care services. Cragg, Andrusyszyn, and Fraser (2005) observed that because the respondents in their study were working or were professional women with good incomes, several reported that they were able to buy services for chores that they could no longer manage themselves. One respondent is quoted as saying, "I spend money on things I could do myself, because the strain of doing everything would be the last straw. I now have a cleaning lady, and I am constantly using services I never did before. Before this I never paid anyone to cut the grass, do mending, or wrap gifts. … We cannot really afford these services, but life would be intolerable for everyone if chores became a point of conflict."

Some women have also used the strategy of doing fewer house chores, especially during the time they have to study for examinations.

Another option for some women is investment in household equipment. New equipment such as washing machines, dishwashers, microwaves, vacuum cleaners, stove and blenders among others have since been manufactured to make household chores easier. One career woman for instance said the type of technology she is looking for is a kind of robot that can do all the chores in the house independently.

Such services and facilities will require budgetary allocations and in some countries could be very expensive, but investment in these available resources could give some space to women to pursue their educational dreams. Also, the qualifications obtained through further education could pay back the expense. Time is the most valuable asset for career and studying women, and at times they have to spend money on some household services and equipment to gain or *buy* time for their studies.

Institutional Support

Much as the home, communal, and workplace supports are crucial for women to succeed in ODL programs, one cannot leave out the technical, counseling, administrative, and tutorial support an ODL institution provides. In view of the possible isolation that students face in ODL programs, which could even lead to dropping out in some cases, and all the other numerous anticipated challenges, most ODL institutions are set up to provide support services for their students. Recognizing that the flexibility in ODL programs is most suitable for women and that as a result more women enroll in ODL programs, institutions have to make conscious efforts to make their support systems women-friendly.

Clear guidelines as to what will be expected of them in the program and whom to call on with what kind of questions and for what kind of help will be useful for students. Because in Ghana students find reading difficult, it will be helpful to give them more information during orientation and emphasize that they have to read their handbooks. A Web site that is updated on a regular basis and text messages to students' cell phones will be other effective ways of staying in touch and giving them all the information they need. Counseling and tutorial services cannot be taken for granted as well. Having counselors and tutors at various learning centers who are on call for students will be helpful.

ICT Support

Emerging information and communication technology has introduced several interactive approaches in ODL programs. ICT has helped to bridge the distance in ODL.

Print materials for distance education remain the most common medium for ODL in developing countries. However, other media such as radio and television broadcasting and audio- and videocassettes are often used as supplements. Telephone and fax are used, often for tutor support. Two-way radio may serve the same function, and there is some limited use of e-mail. Face-to-face sessions at study centers may complement these media.

Any significant use of new ICTs such as audio-conferencing and videoconferencing, as well as computer-based communication (e-mail, Web access, and online learning), currently is restricted in usage in the developing countries. Much as women have been found to be technology unfriendly, ICT packages for distance learning will provide a good support for women if it is made women friendly. This aspect has been looked at in detail in the next chapter. Figure 22 illustrates women's situations in ODL programs and how they could be supported.

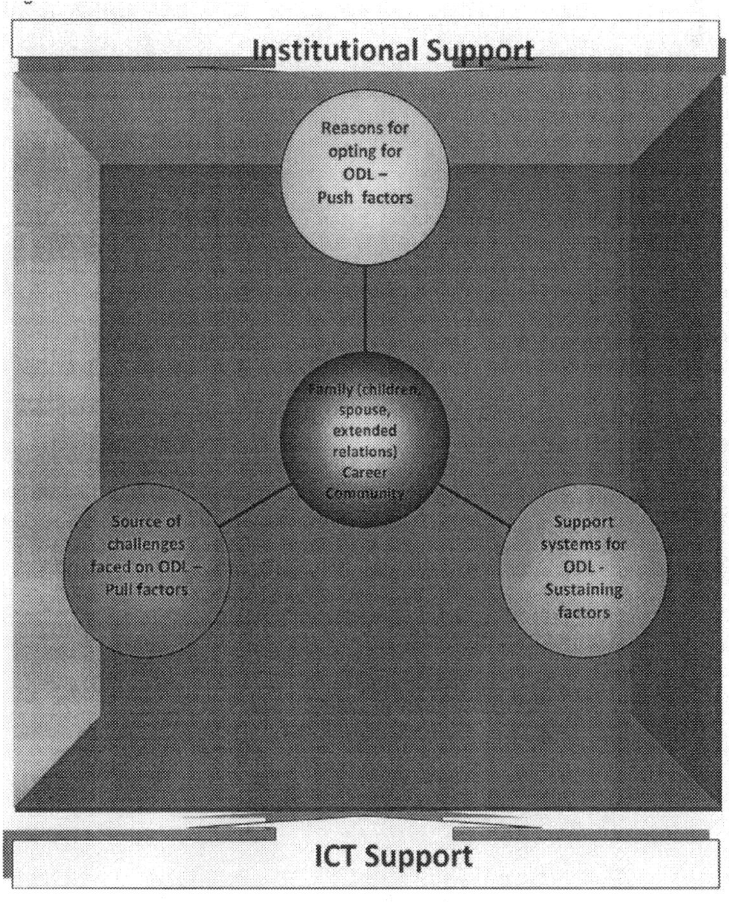

Fig. 22 Model of Women in ODL

This chapter has explored the potential of ODL for widening access to education for women. The flexibility that ODL offers makes it possible for women, most of whom may otherwise not able to leave their family, young children, and work, to engage in further studies. By studying at a distance, most women are able to take care of their multiple roles. Most spouses have also found it convenient and have fully supported their wives based on the assurance that the distance learning program will not take them away from home. Meanwhile it is interesting to note that the very factors that push women to opt for distance learning are the same factors that challenge them most—family (spouse and children), communal commitments (services for extended family and other community roles), and work (paid jobs). These factors make it difficult for women to sail through their distance learning programs. In some instances it becomes so oppressive that women have to give up their life dreams of obtaining a degree or pursuing some career goals through education. However, it is exciting to note that the same factors that push women to opt for distance learning and pose challenges to them in the process can serve as their most effective support systems to succeed in the programs. In addition to providing support systems and exploring the potential of ICT, the approval and support of husbands, children, extended families, communities, and workplaces should not in any way be taken for granted if women are to succeed in their distance learning endeavors.

Chapter 10

Tying the Knots: ICT for ODL for Women

Women have been found to learn differently. Like men, their experiences and responsibilities in life inform the way they learn. Frydenberg (2007) has noted that unlike young undergraduate students, adults, especially female students participating in continuing professional education, naturally face life circumstances that emerge from personal, family, home, financial, and community commitments that have a significant effect on their studies. Hence they need a mode that will respond to and help them cope with their life circumstances.

The opportunities that information and communication technology (ICT) offer make it worth considering supporting the studies of women in ODL programs. It is true that women have been noted as not being fond of technology. They have also been found to have limited access to technology, especially in developing countries. But in view of the tremendous potential of ICTs in meeting their learning needs, especially at a distance, conscious effort has to be made to make ICT highly accessible and women-friendly (GenARDIS n.d.; Holloway and Savvina 2008; Leinonen, Smith, and Haataja 2006; Sales, Al-Barwani, and Miske 2007).

The rapid pace of development of ICT and the potential that it presents has directed the education and entire development policies of most countries and quite recently that of the developing world to make education highly accessible. Most policies of education in developing countries are exploring ways of utilizing the full potential of ICT to reach out to both the privileged and the marginalized in education. In spite of the argument that developing countries need "bread" more than "computers," the potential of ICT for bridging the divides in society and the developed and developing world cannot be overlooked. Ignoring the crucial role of ICT in bridging the educational divides could result in a more disastrous widening of socioeconomic divides in society (South Africa 2008; Kyama and Waititu 2008; Abdon, Raab, and Ninomiya 2008; Dalvit, Thinyane, Muyingi, and Terzoli 2007; Gurstein, M. 2007; Maplecroft maps 2006).

ICT FOR ODL

ICT has led a revolution in education, especially in ODL. Technology, rapidly developing as it is, has dictated the pace of growth of ODL and will continue to do so. Because ODL thrives on ICT, the advancement in technology gives direction to ODL. As a result ODL has progressed from correspondence education to distance education to technology-mediated learning or virtual education (Mangesi 2007; Mitchell and Murugan 2000; McIsaac and Gunawardena 1996; May 1994).

The potential of ICT for education is in vogue, especially in developing countries. Country policies are full of strategies for utilizing the potential of ICT for promoting equitable access in education. The use of ICT to facilitate teaching and learning in the face-to-face mode and at a distance has therefore become a global practice (ICT Summit 2009; Kumar 2008; Latchem, Maru, and Alluri 2004; Lindsay 2002). Hargis notes that "Throughout time, humans have utilized different technological tools to enhance both basic communication and learning. For instance, humans have gone from cave drawings to web sites; from petroglyphics to blogging; from conversations to instant messaging; and from storytelling to podcasting" (Hargis 2008). Prummer (2007) also notes that the use of media and technology has contributed to the changes that the term *distance education* has undergone since the beginnings in the mid-1800s.

Yousuf, Anwar, and Sarwar (2008) have explained distance learning as situations in which learners are physically separated from educational providers, communicating in writing by postal mail, e-mail, fax, or computer conferencing; verbally by telephone, audio-conferencing, or videoconferencing; or in periodic tutorial sessions. This implies that in distance learning the teacher and the learner reside at separate locations and technology is used for interaction between them or to bridge the communication gap (Middlehurst and Woodfield 2003; Mkoka 2009). In using ICT for education, four interconnected characteristics of advanced technologies have been noted by Baryamureeba (2007). The first is their capacity for interactivity. Thus ICT offers effective two-way communication on a one-to-one or one-to-many basis. Second, ICTs are available twenty-four hours a day in real time, synchronous or asynchronous. Third, ICT through its interconnected infrastructure now has a reach over geographic distances that were not possible even in the recent past. The fourth feature of the current innovations in ICT is the continuing reduction in the relative costs of communicating, although this differs by location. Such a system that facilitates the teaching-learning enterprise is thus relevant and applicable not only to the developed world but also the developing world

In the light of the various developments in ICT and their impact on ODL, Bates has defined three generations of ODL as follows:

- First-generation learners studied alone, with limited contact from the educational provider. This model was typically used for correspondence study and is still used to provide learners with resources they can study independently to prepare for examinations offered by an accrediting body, such as a professional organization or university.
- Second-generation distance education provides learning resources in one or more media and consistent communication between the learner and the tutor and, sometimes, additional learning support from the educational provider. This approach is used in many situations in which distance learners study alone, rather than in groups.
- Third-generation distance learning provides learning resources in one or more media and interaction among learners as well as between the tutor and learner. Interaction may be via conferencing technologies (audio, video, computer), e-mail, or face-to-face meetings and is used when group learning is combined with individual learning. (Bates in COL 2004b)

These generational phases show how ICT has changed the face of the delivery of ODL to enhance its interactivity. Thus technology has influenced the evolution of learning, which has led to the global recognition that e-learning can help address issues of educational equity and social exclusion, and open up democratic and accessible educational opportunities. The influence of ICT on education at a distance has contributed to its description with terms such as *open and distance learning, technology-mediated learning, e-learning, online learning,* and *virtual campus,* all of which could be used interchangeably to mean one thing—the use of ICT to deliver education (Barlow and Zackmann 2008; Bates 1997; Perraton 1997; Bullen 1999; Hope 2006; ICT 2009; Kumar 2008).

Through the Internet, ICT provides academics with an opportunity to create rich learning environments for their students. The ready access to multimedia at one's desktop provides the opportunity to develop engaging and interactive learning resources to enhance even traditional learning environments (Gulati 2008). Describing electronic academic courses as *multimodal courses*, Birch and Sankey (2008) explain that *multimodal courses* involve the use of multimedia and ICT to develop dynamic course resources that appeal to different sensory modes and a variety of learning styles. In detail, a multimodal course may include elements such as simulations, interactive diagrams, images, video and audio materials, interactive quizzes and crosswords, PowerPoint lectures with audio, and hyperlinked examples. The advances in ICT, such as the Internet as a major source of global information, have also encouraged educators to develop rich and technology-based learning environments at all levels of education. In view of this, governments and non-governmental agencies that fund educational endeavors in developing countries have advocated the use of new technologies to reduce the cost of reaching and educating large numbers of children and adults, whether male or female, who are currently missing out on education mostly through ODL (Gulati 2008; Farrel, Isaacs, and Trucano 2007; Farrel and Shafika 2007; Farrel 2004; Farrel 2003).

The introduction of e-learning designed to help students facilitate learning processes is removing distance constraints and changing interpersonal communication dynamics (Kim 2008). Birch and Sankey (2008) explain that in the use of the Internet for teaching and learning, students process information electronically rather than through face-to-face contact with others such as teachers and other students or through traditional paper-based modes of expression and communication. The use of the Internet for teaching and learning at a distance implies teacher-directed learning activities using computers, completing and submitting assignments electronically, participating in group chats involving near-simultaneous written dialogue, and obtaining teacher feedback electronically. In this process learners organize their learning independently, which makes them take over some of the roles of the instructor (Annand 2007; Arinto 2007). The use of Internet tools, for instance in a teaching-learning process, facilitates a high level of interaction among learners that help to overcome the isolation in distance learning. Because greater emphasis is placed on student interaction and reflection, e-learning has been found to be better than the purely print-based distance learning courses (Wong 2008; Lindsay 2002; Latchem, Maru, and Alluri 2004; Magagula 2002).

Distance learning therefore encompasses and relies on the use of information technology to make learning more productive and more individualized; it gives instruction a more scientific base, makes it appropriate and more effective, more immediate, and makes access to resources more equal most especially for women. By using connected communication tools both male and female students can decide about their studies where and when they can best learn and how to use resources in a more convenient way. They can also work in more supportive environments, seek help from tutors and colleagues, and share their learning experiences and ideas in a cosmetic and productive fashion (Hussain and Safdar 2008; Albirini 2008).

ICTs for education are being advanced every day. New innovations keep emerging, which continuously increases the opportunity to minimize the distance in ODL (Gulati 2008). In Table 36, Mitra (2008) presents detailed information on various ICT facilities and how they could be used to provide basic support in ODL programs.

Table 36 ICT Usage and Benefits

Available ICT	Used for	Benefits
Telephone and cell phones	• Individual and one-to-one interaction: phone calls and brief SMS messages • Small group interaction: telephone conferencing when a number of telephones are connected	• Reasonable cost • Easy access • Needs-based
E-mail	• Communication may be to one student or to a whole group • Students can choose when to reply	• Fast • Inexpensive • Can transmit material of all kinds through attached documents
Bulletin Boards	• Distributing tutorial notes • Exchange information for group projects • For briefing, asking questions or commenting on a topic	• Fast • Sharing Information • Group interaction • Inexpensive
Online Discussion Forums	• Synchronous computer conferencing that brings a group together to discuss a specific topic • Asynchronous discussions allow students to join in and express their views at any time	• Real-time event (synchronous) • Any time interaction (asynchronous) • Freedom from fixed location
Video Conferencing	For interaction at multiple sites where there is an opportunity for ODL tutors and students to see and hear each other	• Direct interaction in real time • Can save huge travel costs

Source Mitra (2008)

Table 36 ICT Usage and Benefits Source Mitra (2008)

Much as ICTs present a lot of potential for both male and female adult learners at a distance, there has been intellectual argument over its ability to promote social presence in a teaching-learning process, recognizing that in traditional classrooms, social presence enhances instructional delivery and the classroom experience. Social presence implies the connections between participants and the tutor to enhance student satisfaction, perceptions of learning, and retention. Various studies have been undertaken to justify the possibility of creating a social presence online. Rahman, Anwar, and Numan (2008), Scollins-Mantha (2008), and Schmieder (2008) have observed that a richer, more engaging learning community can be formed in the online learning classroom.

Online communities are created to fulfill the human need for social interaction with peers and instructors in an online class. A study by Green, van Gyn, Moehr, Lau, and Coward (2004) cited by Schmieder (2008) indicates that students agreed that seven of the nine functions provided by the Web-based online course management system enhanced their learning in the following ways: private e-mail (92.3 percent), calendaring (88.5 percent), course notes (88.5 percent), discussion forums (84.5 percent), online grades (84.5 percent), assignment descriptions (80.8 percent), and online quizzes (80.8 percent). Rahman, Anwar, and Numan (2008) have also observed in a study that e-mail and other Internet programs are effective tools for interaction as well as to make a bridge of communication between both tutors and learners. In their study most of the learners (94 percent) gave their opinions that e-mail technologies support the teachers or tutors to consult in a better way, and almost 82 percent of learners showed eagerness to communicate with teachers by e-mail.

ICT for Supporting Women in ODL

To this point one can emphasize that the potentials of ICT, most especially the Internet, for facilitating interaction at a distance, creating artificial social presence, and widening access to education for women especially to help bridge the gender divide in education at the tertiary level cannot be underestimated. Birch and Sankey (2008) have confirmed that the potential benefits of e-learning include cost-effectiveness, enhanced responsiveness to changing circumstances, consistency, timely content, accessibility, and more rapid feedback, all of which provide customer value and widen access to education.

With the potential of ICTs, distance education institutions are able to offer chances for women to combine distance course with their family responsibilities. It is assumed that distance learners are *autonomous* and *independent* learners who more or less study on their own and work their way through the course materials provided by the institution. The situation differs for female students. Female distance students have shown more interest in support and connectedness with other students and in dealings between students and academic staff. Unlike their male colleagues, they are oriented toward creating opportunities for meeting and working with other students. The study of Plummer (2000; 2004) has found that the demands women make on institutions are different from those of male students and that they value and utilize the services in a different way. Women also place a higher value on local support services; as a result they have a higher rate of attendance at study centers, even though they have to overcome more obstacles to be able to participate. This female-oriented approach to learning at a distance needs to be taken into account by ODL systems that want to provide equal opportunities for men and women (Burge and Lenskyj 1990; Burksh 2007; Care and Sonia 2000; Carlson 2001; Cohoon and Aspray 2006).

Much as women distance learners find support services very useful for their success in ODL programs, the excessive demands of their reproductive and domestic roles become hindrances to their quest for and full usage of available student support systems. If the tutorials and group work take place outside their homes, workplace, or communities, women find it very challenging to make time to attend the tutorials or participate in the study groups they desire so much. The everyday lives of family women are characterized by a degree of chaos and constant interruptions, where the mother is at the beck and call of her children and her partner and their immediate needs, which tend to take precedence over the woman's desire for uninterrupted and concentrated study time. Meanwhile it is assumed that most women in unpaid family work have time on their hands and are free in how they organize their schedules. Studies have shown that only a minority of women distance students do not work outside the home at all. Most of them are in full-time or part-time work in addition to fulfilling their commitments as housewives and mothers. They therefore face difficulty in organizing their studies. Whereas female students have difficulties making time and finding space for their studies, with the support of their spouses men are more likely to be granted the space and privacy needed to pursue their distance courses (Hope 2006; Rekkedal 1994; Rooy 2008; Ramanujam 1997; Spencer 1994; Wall 2004). In discussing women's experiences of distance education, a study by Burge (1990) notes that the women agreed that distance study "isn't for everyone" and that it is a significantly different experience for female learners than it is for male learners. The women under study were grateful that communications technologies, despite their imperfections, allowed them to study from their own homes and at times most convenient to their personal schedules (Green and Trevor-Deutsch 2002).

Considering their busy lifestyles and their desire for collaborative learning, ICT becomes critical for women who are engaged in distance learning. ICT-based learning tends to meet the learning style of females. In a study by Priebe, Ross, and Low (2008) that focused on the use of television for delivery, respondents emphasized that distance learning provided the only option for them to incorporate university study into their busy lifestyles. All the respondents indicated that they would be unlikely to complete their degrees without the option of distance delivery. Unlike young undergraduate students, female students participating in continuing professional education naturally face life circumstances that emerge from personal, family, home, financial, and community commitments that have a significant effect on their studies. Hence they need a mode that will respond and help them cope with their life circumstances (Frydenberg 2007; Wong 2008). In another study where the majority were adults who had been taking courses over a period of years while working and tending to family responsibilities, Gouge

(2008) has noted that female adult learners, especially, can have specific motivation and access issues that are facilitated by forums, chat rooms, e-mail, and other online activities that foster a spirit of community.

Research on women's learning styles has explored the extent of women's independence or connectedness in learning at a distance (Care and Sonia 2000; Hipp 1997; May 1994; Grace 1994; Cragg 1991). Although some studies have proved that women can learn independently, the need for collaborative learning among women has been strongly emphasized. These observations give an indication that given the complex nature of their lifestyles, with the addition of a third shift when they engage in formal studies, it will be most appropriate to adopt a multi-sectorial approach to meet women's learning needs. This is more critical in the distance learning mode. The support systems in ODL programs must be such that they meet the differential learning needs of both sexes. Thus a gender-friendly approach must be adopted.

In the case of women ICT ensures even distribution of resources. According to Care and Sonia (2000) women's ways tend to suggest that, by nature or socialization, women have preferences for cooperative, caring, and connected approaches to learning and working. Feminist educators view collaboration as a fundamental principle and as an important teaching strategy. Collaborative learning practices are seen to promote contact, dialogue, and interaction. In a feminist context, collaborative learning involves sharing power, responsibility, and experience, and a valuing of active participation and egalitarian principles. And this could be obtained in what they term computer-based instruction.

The authors elaborate that cooperative learning in computer-based instruction has produced positive outcomes:

- Students work faster and are better able to apply factual information.

- Students tend to use each other as resources and to motivate each other.
- Students tend to learn from each other and imitate each other's behaviors.
- Students are also more altruistic toward teammates.

If connected communication tools are used, female students could decide about their studies, learning time, place, and resources in a more convenient way. They will also be able to work in more supportive environments. Because the Internet and other ICT packages present a lot of potential for interactive teaching and learning and women distance students tend to prefer connected learning styles, the Internet will offer women opportunities for exchange and cooperation (Kwapong 2007; Scollins-Mantha 2008). By using ICT tools such as phone calls, e-mail, and text messages, women will be able to seek instant help from their teachers and colleagues and share their learning experiences and ideas at regular intervals (Hussain and Safdar 2008; Wong 2008). Researchers who defend the potential of ICT for women are of the view that women no longer have the luxury of ignoring it, since globalization of information and economies are supported by ICT. Recent research suggests that poor citizens from low-income countries could benefit dramatically from having access to telephony, information, and disaster warning systems (Philip 1993; Perraton 1997; Pym 1992; Rathore, Singh, Sunil, and Dubey 1996; Rawaf and Simmons 1992).

In Care and Sonia's study (2000), they found that in women's experiences of online courses that enhance flexibility, the online students had these observations to share:

- [The course] provided flexibility and the opportunity to participate while working and juggling home responsibilities.
- The course design fit my busy lifestyle.

- I could enjoy the course in the comfort of my own home.

Challenges

In spite of the tremendous potential that the Internet presents for distance learning, most especially for women, there are massive challenges that cannot be ignored, especially for women in the developing world. Doubts about the possibility of having a social presence, poverty, political upheaval, high levels of illiteracy, unreliable access to electricity, low levels of ownership of computers, telephone lines, radios, televisions, and access to the Internet affect women's full access to and utilization of ICT (Daly 2003; Hafkin 2003; Huyer and Sikoska 2003; UNESCO 2003; Women's net 2005; World Bank n.d.).

Much as a majority of those in Sonia and Care's study expressed that they enjoyed the chance to reflect on thoughts before they got online and some even wanted more online discussions, some of the students missed the interaction in a classroom environment. They were not comfortable with the lack of a relationship with a tutor and not seeing facial expressions or hearing the tone of voice of the professor or classmates. These are some of the genuine problems that students experience in technology-mediated programs. Wall (2004) found in his study that most students were very teacher dependent.

Women's access to and control over ICT is not equal to that of men. *Access* has been explained to mean the ability to make use of the technology as well as the information and knowledge it provides, whereas *control* refers to the ability to decide how the ICT is used and who can have access to it. African women have been found to lag behind their male counterparts in access to the Internet and its usage. In most parts, women users are part of a small, educated urban elite. Statistics compiled from the International Telecommunication Union World Telecommunication report for 2002 on female

Internet users for 2000 revealed that 16 percent of women in Ethiopia, 25 percent in Morocco, 14 percent in Senegal, and 49 percent in South Africa use the Internet. Meanwhile the situation is different in the United States, where women make up 51 percent of all Internet users (UNESCO 2003; Bisnath 2004; Girard 2003; Hixon, Keller, Bonk, and Ehman 2008).

Infrastructure that provides ICT is a major issue in the third world. Disparities in infrastructure provision are evident across international boundaries, and across developed and developing countries. It is estimated that one-third of the world's population has yet to make a phone call, and less than one-fifth has experienced the Internet. These figures illustrate the lack of telecommunications service to largely poor and predominantly rural peoples in different countries, of whom a great number are women (UNESCO 2003).

In addition to infrastructural drawbacks, the position of women makes them face several inhibitions in accessing the full potential of ICT. The United Nations places lack of access to information as the third most important issue facing women globally, after poverty and violence against them. Low levels of formal education and income among women; multiple roles, which reduces their time for leisure; women's predominance in rural communities; and other socio-cultural factors affect women's access to ICT and its use (Huyer and Sikoska 2003; Rwangoga and Baryayetunga 2007).

Technology is also socially construed. Following international trends, the Ghanaian culture and for that matter the African culture has construed ICT to be gender-specific. Computing remains a heavily male-dominated field even after twenty-five years of extensive efforts to promote female participation (Cohoon and Bill 2006). Telecommunications and computer engineering have largely been considered predominantly men's work, whereas data entry is mainly assigned to women. This may be because of the science and technical nature of the ICT system, which is generally viewed as masculine. The low ratios of girls in science and technology courses in Africa reinforce the negative dynamics that limit women's access to decision-making positions in the fields of science and technology and manage ICT systems (Daly 2003; UNESCO 2003; Hafkin 2003; Bisnath 2004; James, Leinonen, Smith, and Haataja 2006; Kwapong 2007).

One other major problem for women in relation to ICT is that they are underrepresented in all decision-making structures in the ICT sector, which generally undermines the negotiation of gender-sensitive investment decisions and the introduction of innovative patterns, policies, and standards in the ICT sector. Women's low share of ICT specialists' jobs has not increased since 1998. In 2005, only 25 percent of all software engineers in the United States were women. On the other hand, the number of women who have relative specialization in computing in Mexico is higher than other countries (World Bank n.d.). For the year 2000 28.5 percent of the computer programmers and systems analysts in the United States were women; women made up 23.4 percent of them in Korea, 18 percent in Germany, and 47.7 percent in Thailand. With this low level of representation, one could wonder about the extent to which women could influence decision-making on ICT design and management issues.

Studies have shown that the manufacture of ICT systems is not gender-friendly (Rumble and Badri 2007; Som 2003; Siaciwena 2000). Hafkin (2003) has noted that only a few Internet resources are available that meets the information needs of women in developing countries in a form they can use. Besides the above, women have also not been fairly treated in terms of portrayal on the Internet. In some cases the Internet has been used for women's sexual exploitation and harassment. There is trafficking of women through the Internet, pornography, sexual harassment, and use of the Internet to perpetuate violence against women. These factors may not encourage women to use the Internet for more serious business such as online learning.

The majority of women are poor, and it is worse in the third world. Most of them also live in rural communities where communication infrastructure is rare. This no doubt limits women's access to ICT facilities for education at a distance. No matter how much cheaper ICT is becoming, there is the need for some financial commitment in utilizing its full potential. Almost all communication facilities cost money. Women are less likely than men to own radios, televisions, and personal computers or to access them when they want to. In most traditional communities, the technology in the home is controlled by the head of the house, who is usually the father, husband, brother, or another male. When it involves paying for information access, such as a rural information center or a cybercafé, women are less likely to have the disposable income to do so. Even in cases where the service might be free, women may have limited access, since in some communities women and men do not share common areas. The few facilities that may be installed in public areas may not be accessible to them (Kwapong 2007). These challenges could limit women's full access to and utilization of ICT tools for educational purposes.

The discussion in this chapter has revealed that for women, ICTs have much potential for facilitating studies at a distance. Women have been found to have a learning style that requires more support services if they are to succeed in distance learning programs. Much as women have found support services useful for their studies, it becomes challenging for them to access support facilities if they take them away from home, work, and all their responsibilities. What will be most useful for women is the kind of facility that takes the support to their doorstep, to be used at their convenience. In view of this, a conscious effort has to be made to make ICT for education at a distance women-friendly and easily accessible. There would no doubt be challenges in the process, but where there is a will, there is a way.

References

Abdon, B., R. Raab, and S. Ninomiya (2008). E-learning for international agriculture development: Dealing with challenges. *International Journal of Education and Development Using ICT* 4 (1).

Abdulkafi, A. (2008). The Internet in developing countries: A medium of economic, cultural and political domination. *International Journal of Education and Development Using ICT* 4 (1).

Abrioux, D. A. M. X. (2008). Structural framework for higher education open and distance learning in Papua New Guinea. Retrieved April 9, 2009, from www.col.org/resources/publications/consultancies/Pages/2008-01-frmwrkPNG.aspx.

Aggrey, E. (2008). Ghana likely to exceed targets for telephone penetration. Retrieved March 3, 2009, from www.pcworld.com/businesscenter/article/147145/ghana_likely_to_exceed_targets_for_telephone_penetration.html.

Aggor, R. A., and P. E. Kinyanjui (1992). Survey on distance education in Ghana. *The Commonwealth of Learning* 56.

Albirini, A. (2008). Wakunga ICT livelihood and education project. Retrieved May 19, 2008, from http://ijedict.dec.uwi.edu/viewarticle.php?id=360&layout=html.

Alghali, E., E. D. A. Turay, E. J. D. Thompson, and B. A. Kandeh (2005). Education in Sierra Leone, with particular reference to open and distance learning and information and communication technologies. Retrieved from May 18, 2009 from www.col.org/SiteCollectionDocuments/05SierraLeone_EnviroScan.pdf.

Alluri, K., and R. Zackmann (2008). Technology-mediated open and distance education for agricultural education and improved livelihoods in Sub-Saharan Africa. Retrieved April 9, 2009, from www.col.org/resources/publications/consultancies/Pages/studyAfrica.aspx.

Amoakohene, I. A. (2005). Advertising and sponsorship trends in the Ghanaian electronic media—An assessment. *Ghana Social Science Journal* 3 (1, 2).

Ampah, S. (2009). Ghana needs access and equity in education to ensure development. Retrieved February 18, 2009, from www.theghanaianjournal.com/2009/01/06/ghana-needs-access-and-equity-in-education-to-ensure-development/.

Annand, D. (2007). Re-organizing universities for the information age. *The International Review of Research in Open and Distance Learning* 8 (3).

Ansere, J. (2002). Issues of distance education in Ghana. *The Ghanaian Chronicle 3(6)*.

Arinto, P. B. (2007). Going the distance: Towards a new professionalism for full-time distance education faculty at the university of the Philippines. *The International Review of Research in Open and Distance Learning* 8 (3).

Asraf, M. M., P. Swatman, and J. Hanisch (2007). Some perspectives on understanding the adoption and implementation of ICT interventions in developing countries. *The Journal of Community Informatics* 3 (4). Retrieved March 15, 2008, from http://ci-journal.net/index.php/ciej/article/view/297/387.

Barlow-Zambodla, A., and F. Adams (2008). Using mobile technology for learner support in open schooling. Retrieved April 9, 2009, from www.col.org/resources/publications/consultancies/Pages/mobileTechnology.aspx.

Baryamureeba, V. (2007). ICT as an engine for Uganda's economic growth: The role of and opportunities for Makerere University. *International Journal of Computing and ICT Research* 1 (1), 47–57. www.ijcir.org/volume1-number1/article6.pdf.

Bates, A. W. T. (1997). Impact of technological change on open and distance learning. Retrieved May 11, 2009, from http://searchcio-midmarket.techtarget.com/sDefinition/0,,sid183_gci509906,00.html.

Beardon, H. (2009). Mobiles for Development—How mobile technologies can enhance plan and partners work in Africa. Retrieved April 6, 2009, from http://en.wikipedia.org/wiki/Information_and_communication_technologies_for_development.

Birch, D., and M. D. Sankey (2008). Drivers for and obstacles to the development of interactive multimodal technology-mediated distance higher education courses. *International Journal of Education and Development Using ICT* 4 (1).

Bisnath, S. (2004). Third meeting of the working group on gender issues. Retrieved March 21, 2008, from www.itu.int/ITU-D/gender/events/3rdAnnualWGGIMeeting/documents/3-11.pdf.

Bruce, D. W., V. Hagens, and K. Ellis (2007). Technology mediated learning: Building capacity in rural communities. *The Journal of Community Informatics* 3 (4). Retrieved March 15, 2008, from http://ci-journal.net/index.php/ciej/article/view/334/381.

Bullen, M. (1990). Learner responses to television in distance education: The need for a qualitative approach to research. In B. Clough (ed.), Proceedings of the ninth annual conference of the Canadian Association for the Study of Adult Education (pp. 48–53). Victoria, BC: University of Victoria.

Burge E. (1990). Women studying in distance education: Issues and principles. *Journal of Distance Education*, 5(1).

Burksh, Q. (2007). Empowerment of women through distance education in Pakistan. *Turkish Online Journal of Distance Education—TOJDE* 8 (4). Retrieved March 20, 2009, from http://tojde.anadolu.edu.tr/tojde28/articles/article_11.htm.

Care, W. D., and A. Sonia (2000). Women in distance education: Overcoming barriers to learning. *New Horizons in Adult Education* 14 (2). Retrieved March 9, 2009, from http://education.fiu.edu/newhorizons/journals/vol14n2.pdf.

Carlson, S. (2001). Distance education. Retrieved March 20, 2009, from Educationhttp://chronicle.com/free/2001/09/2001090501u.htm.

CAPA (n.d.). Improving access and equity for postgraduates from rural and isolated areas. Retrieved April 11, 2009, from www.capa.edu.au/briefing-papers/2003-11-30/improving-access-and-equity-postgraduates-rural-and-isolated-areas. Centre for Continuing Education (2006). University of Cape Coast, Ghana.

Chen, M., and L. Chen (2008). Development of equal opportunities to education using ICT: overview of the nationwide project on modern distance education for schools in the rural areas of China. *Asian Journal of Distance Education* 6 (2), 12–16. Retrieved April 18, 2009, from www.distanceandaccesstoeducation.org/contents/AJDE2008_Chen.pdf.

Cohoon, M., and W. Bill (2006). Women and information technology. Retrieved April 15, 1009, from http://search.barnesandnoble.com/Women-and-Information-Technology/J-McGrath-Cohoon/e/9780262033459#TABS.

Cohoon, J. M., and W. Aspray (2006). Women and information technology: Research on underrepresentation. Retrieved March 29, 2009, from http://mitpress.mit.edu/catalog/item/default.asp?ttype=2&tid=10924.

COL (n.d.). Open and distance learning for development. Retrieved May 11, 2007, from www.col.org/colweb/site/pid/2963.

COL (2000). The use of information and communications technology (ICT) in learning and distance education. Retrieved April 6, 2009, from www.col.org/SiteCollectionDocuments/00intelecon.pdf.

COL (2002). Distance education and open learning in Sub-Saharan Africa—A literature survey on policy and practice. Retrieved April 9, 2009, from www.col.org/SiteCollectionDocuments/02DEinSSA_LiteratureSurvey.pdf.

COL (2004a). Costing distance education and open learning in Sub-Saharan Africa. Retrieved April 9, 2009, from www.col.org/SiteCollectionDocuments/04CostingDEinSSA.pdf.

COL (2004b). Towards a strategy on developing African teacher capabilities in the use of information and communication technology. Retrieved April 9, 2009, from www.col.org/resources/publications/consultancies/Pages/2004-10-teachCapabilities.aspx.

COL (2007). Developing digital content. Retrieved April 9, 2009, from www.col.org/resources/publications/consultancies/Pages/2007-09-14.aspx.

COL (2008). Using mobile technology for learner support in open schooling. Retrieved April 7, 2009, from www.col.org/SiteCollectionDocuments/Mobile%20Technology_Final%20Report.pdf.

Commission of the European Communities (2006). EU *Commission* Progress Report *2006.* Retrieved March 23, 2009, from http://ec.europa.eu/enlargement/pdf/key_documents/2006/Nov/tr_sec_1390_en.pdf.

Considine, G., I. Watson, and R. Hall (2005). Who's missing out? Access and equity in vocational education and training. Retrieved February 15, 2009, from www.ncver.edu.au/research/proj/nr3009.pdf; www.ncver.edu.au/publications/1611.html.

Cookson, P. S. (2002). Access and Equity in distance education: Research and development and quality concerns. Retrieved May 11, 2009, from http://redie.uabc.mx/vol4no2/contents-cookson.html; http://74.125.77.132/search?q=cache:IiQ84O3zW2QJ:edu581-2-s08.wikispaces.com/file/view/accessandequity(2).ppt+what+is+access+and+equity+in+education&hl=it&ct=clnk&cd=26&gl=it.

Cragg, C. E. B. (1991). Nurses' experiences of a distance course by correspondence and audio-teleconference. *The Journal of Distance Education* 6 (2).

Cragg, C. E. B., M. Andrusyszyn, and J. Fraser (2005). Sources of support for women taking professional programs by distance education. *Journal of Distance Education* 20(1), 21–38.

Creed, C., T. Allsop, R. Mills, and R. Morpheth (2005). The art of the possible: issues of learner support in open and distance learning in low income countries. Retrieved April 9, 2009, from www.col.org/resources/publications/consultancies/Pages/2005-03-possible.aspx.

Daly, J. (2003). ICT, gender equality and empowering women. Retrieved March 20, 2008, from http://topics.developmentgateway.org/ict/sdm/previewDocument.do~activeDocumentId=622821.

Dalvit, L., M. Thinyane, H. Muyingi, and A. Terzoli (2007). The deployment of an e-commerce platform and related projects in a rural area in South Africa. *International Journal of Computing and ICT Research* 1 (1), 9–18. www.ijcir.org/issue1/article 2.

Dassin, J. (n.d.). Promoting access and equity in post-graduate education: The Ford Foundation International Fellowships Program. Retrieved May 20, 2009, from www.nuffic.nl/pdf/os/em/dassin.pdf.

Demiray, E., and S. Curabay (2000). Distance education for women's development: A case study at Anadolu University, Turkey. *Malaysian Journal of Distance Education* 2 (2).

Denison, T., and G. Johanson (2007). Surveys of the use of information and communications technologies by community-based organizations. *The Journal of Community Informatics* 3 (2). Retrieved March 15, 2008, from http://ci-journal.net/index.php/ciej/article/view/316/356.

Dikshit, H. P., S. Garg, S. Panda, and N. Vijayshri (2002). *Access and equity: Challenges for open and distance learning*. New Delhi: Vedam Books.

Dodds, T. (1996). The use of distance education in non-formal education. Retrieved April 12, 2009, from www.col.org/resources/publications/consultancies/Pages/1997-disabledindia.aspx.

Dunlop, C. C. (2004a). Evaluation report: COL-African virtual university e-learning workshop. Retrieved April 9, 2009, from www.col.org/SiteCollectionDocuments/04eLearning_Kenya.pdf.

Dunlop, C. C. (2004b). Evaluation report, executive summary and highlights: Third Pan-Commonwealth forum on open learning (PCF3). Retrieved April 9, 2009, from www.col.org/SiteCollectionDocuments/04PCF3.pdf.

Education Reforms (2007). Ghana education reforms. Retrieved March 2, 2009, from www.ghana.gov.gh/ghana/education_reform_2007_glance.jsp.

Effeh, E. (1991). Determinants of the study patterns of female distant learners: An evaluative survey. *The Journal of Distance Education* 6 (2), 58–63.

Evans, K. (1995). Barriers to participation of women in technological education and the role of distance education. *The Commonwealth of Learning.* Retrieved December 15, 2008 from www.col.org/barriers.htm.

Faith, K. (1988). Toward new horizons for women in distance education: International perspectives. Retrieved March 14, 2009, from http://books.google.com.mx/books?hl=en&id=vAcOAAAAQAAJ&dq=Toward+new+Horizons+For+Women+in+Distance+Education:+international+perspectives&printsec=frontcover&source=web&ots=gV_AGofhmW&sig=Zf_tD2KKF2Xtoj8mUMStMoE3Z20&sa=X&oi=book_result&resnum=1&ct=result.

Faith, K., and J. Sturrock (1990). Women and university distance education in Canada. Retrieved March 22, 2009, from www.nald.ca/litweb/other/cclow/newslet/1990/March_v7/15.htm.

Farrell, G. (2003). A virtual university for small states of the commonwealth. Retrieved April 9, 2009, from www.col.

org/resources/publications/consultancies/Pages/2003-10-VUSSC.aspx.

Farrel, G. (2004). ICT and literacy: Who benefits? - Experience from Zambia and India. Retrieved April 9, 2009, from www.col.org/resources/publications/consultancies/Pages/2004-09-ICT.aspx.

Farrel, G., S. Isaacs, and M. Trucano (2007). The NEPAD e-schools demonstration project: A work in progress. Retrieved April 9, 2009, from www.col.org/resources/publications/consultancies/Pages/2007-09-NEPAD.aspx.

Farrell, G., and I. Shafika (2007). Survey of ICT and education in Africa: A summary report, based on 53 country surveys. Retrieved April 6, 2009, from www.infodev.org/en/Publication.353.html.

Fontaine, G. (2002). Presence in "Teleland." In Rudestam, K. E., and J. Schoenholtz-Read, eds. *Handbook of online learning—innovations in higher education and corporate training*. London: Sage Publications.

Frydenberg, J. (2007). Persistence in university continuing education online classes. *The International Review of Research in Open and Distance Learning* 8 (3).

GenARDIS (n.d.). Gender and agriculture/rural development in the information society. Retrieved May 11, 2008, from www.apcwomen.org/genardis/.

Ghana (n.d.). Ghana information and communications technology directorate (GICTeD). Retrieved April 9, 2009, from www.moc.gov.gh/index.php.

Ghana (2008). General news: Ministry to encourage more women to venture into ICT. Retrieved March 17, 2008, from http://lcweb2.loc.gov/cgi-bin/query/r?frd/cstdy:@field(DOCID+gh0079).

Ghana (2007a). Ghana's education system. Retrieved April 14, 2008, from www.ghana.gov.gh/ghana/education_reform_2007_glance.jsp; www.ghana.gov.gh/schools_and_universities; www.ghana.gov.gh/ghanas_education_system; www.ghana.gov.gh/schools_and_universities.

Ghana (2007b). Ghana's education system. Retrieved April 14, 2008, from http://www.ghana.gov.gh/schools_and_universities; http://www.ghana.gov.gh/ghanas_education_system.

Ghana (2006). The Ghana ICT for Accelerated Development (ICT4AD) policy. Retrieved March 3, 2009, from www.comminit.com/redirect.cgi?m=6ae4e65542c99f8be1f6abbb7cf63db6.

Ghana (2004). Republic of Ghana—National ICT Policy and Plan Development Committee. Retrieved March 31, 2008, from www.ict.gov.gh/html/Landscape%20of%20ICT%20Human%20Resources%20&%20Expertise%20.htm.

Ghana (2003a). Developing effective markets for the golden age of business: National Medium Term Private Sector Development Strategy 2004–2008, Vol. 1. Retrieved May 11, 2008, from www.ghana.gov.gh/pbcopin/nmtp.pdf.

Ghana (2003b). Ghana poverty reduction strategy 2003–2005—An agenda for growth and prosperity. Retrieved February 16, 2008, from http://poverty.worldbank.org/files/Ghana_PRSP.pdf.

Ghana (2002). Meeting the challenges of education in the twenty first century—Report of the president's committee on review of education reforms in Ghana. Accra: Education, Adwinsa Publications (Gh) Ltd.

Ghanaweb (n.d.). Education in Ghana. www.ghanaweb.com/GhanaHomePage/.

Girard, B. (2003). The challenges of ICTs and rural radio—Expert consultation on rural women and distance learning: Regional strategies. Retrieved December 10, 2007, from www.fao.org/sd/2003/PE12033a_en.htm.

GLSS 4 (2000). Ghana living standards survey—report of the fourth round, Ghana Statistical Service.

Grace, M. (1994). Meanings and motivations: women's experiences of studying at a distance. *The Journal of Open and Distance Learning* 9 (1).

Gouge, C. (2008). Redesigning online instruction: Theory and application. *International Journal of Instructional Technology and Distance Learning* 5 (2).

Gulati, S. (2008). Technology-enhanced learning in developing nations: A review. *The International Review of Research in Open and Distance Learning* 9 (1).

Gurstein, M. (2007). Some thoughts on ICTs in a developing world context. *The Journal of Community Informatics* 3 (4).

Hafkin, N. J. (2003). Joint UNECE/UNCTAD/UIS/ITU/OECD/EUROSTAT statistical workshop: Monitoring the information society: Data, measurement and methods—

gender issues in ICT statistics and indicators, with particular emphasis on developing countries. Retrieved March 21, 2008, from www.unece.org/stats/documents/ces/sem.52/3.e.pdf.

Hargis, J. (2008). A second life for distance learning. *Turkish Online Journal of Distance Education—TOJDE* 9 (2/1).

Hipp, H. (1997). Women studying at a distance: what do they need to succeed? *The Journal of Open and Distance Learning* 12 (2).

Hixon, E., J. B. Keller, C. J. Bonk, and L. H. Ehman (2008). Professional development that increases technology integration by K–12 teachers: Influence of the TICKIT Program. *International Journal of Instructional Technology and Distance Learning* 5 (3).

Holloway, K., and C. Savvina (2008). Teaching with instructional television, *International Journal of Instructional Technology and Distance Learning* 5 (1), 17–24.

Hui, Y. (1989). The impacts of ICT based education on the informational literacy of teachers and students in Beijing rural districts. Retrieved May 11, 2009, from www.editlib.org/?fuseaction=Reader.NoAccess&paper_id=25375.

Hussain, I., and M. Safdar (2008). Role of information technologies in teaching learning process: Perception of the faculty. *Turkish Online Journal of Distance Education—TOJDE* 9 (2).

Huyer S., & Sikoska T., (2003). Overcoming the gender digital divide—Understanding ICTs and their potential for the empowerment of women: INSTRAW Research Paper Series No. 1. Retrieved March 21, 2008, from INSTRAW database.

Hope, A. (2006). Factors for success in dual mode institutions. Retrieved April 9, 2009, from www.col.org/resources/publications/consultancies/Pages/2006-dualMode.aspx.

ICT Summit (2009). Summary of research results. Retrieved April 28, 2009, from http://neuf.cprost.sfu.ca/foundations/presentations/ICTSummit2009.pdf.

Infoplease (n.d.). Ghana. Retrieved March 10, 2008, from www.infoplease.com/ipa/A0107584.html.

ITU (2007). United Nations Conference on Trade and Development—Beyond WSIS: World Information Society Report.

ITU (2009). ITU Telecom World 2009. Retrieved June 9, 2009, from www.itu.int/WORLD2009/.

Jefferson, T. (2007). Some historical factors that led to access and equity in education. Retrieved May 1, 2009, from http://edu581-2-s08.wikispaces.com/file/view/accessandequity(2).ppt.

Jeffries, M. (1999). Research in distance education. *Journal of Distance Education* 14 (1), 102–114.

James, T., E. Leinonen, R. Smith, and M. Haataja (2006). A manual of possible interventions to improve the situation of women in high-level ICTs in South Africa. Retrieved March 21, 2008 from http://women-in-ict.meraka.csir.co.za/images/b/b5/Manual_print.pdf.

Kanwar, A. S. (1990). Distance education for women's equality: An Indian perspective. *Journal of Distance Education* 5 (2).

Kasday, L. R., and L. Noble (2000). *Culture in the communication age.* Retrieved April 17, 2009, from www.webuse.umd.edu/Webuse_References.htm.

Kasday, L. R. (2001). Access and equity in web based education: ATAP's policy recommendations. Retrieved April 12, 2009, from www.csun.edu/cod/conf/2001/proceedings/0156salomaa.htm2001.

Kasozi, A. B. K. (n.d.). .Access and equity to higher education in Uganda: Whose children attend university and are paid for by the state? Retrieved April 14, 2009 from http://ahero.uwc.ac.za/index.php?module=cshe&action=downloadfile&fileid=36807145012339262082233.

Keegan, D. (1990). Theoretical principles of distance education. Routledge, New York.

Kim, M. (2008). Factors influencing the acceptance of e-learning courses for mainstream faculty in higher institutions. *International Journal of Instructional Technology and Distance Learning* 5 (2).

King, B. (2006). Access and equity in distance education. Retrieved April 12, 2009, from www.uned.ac.cr/XIVCongreso/memoria/pdf%20expertos/Conferencia%20Greville%20Rumble.pdf; http://ec.europa.eu/education/policies/2010/doc/comm481_en.pdf.

Kirkpatrick, C. (2005). Presto-chango! Transforming an instructional video into an interactive DVD. Panel presentation for Purdue University Teaching Learning and Technology conference.

Kirkup, G. and C. V. Prummer (1990). Support and connectedness: The needs of women distance education students. *Journal of Distance Education* 5 (2), 9–31.

Koul, B. N. and A. Kanwar (2006). Perspectives on distance education towards a culture of quality. Retrieved March 20, 2008, from www.col.org/worldreview/volume6.htme.

Kramarae, C. (2001). The third shift—women learning online. Retrieved March 20, 2009, from www.aauw.org/research/upload/thirdshift.pdf.

Kumar, K. (2008). Education for a Digital World—*Virtual design studios: Solving learning problems in developing countries.* Retrieved April 6, 2009, from http://www.colfinder.org/materials/Education_for_a_Digital_World/Education_for_a_Digital_World_part1.pdf; http://74.125.77.132/search?q=cache:uhWAY29iouAJ:www.colfinder.org/materials/Education_for_a_Digital_World/Education_for_a_Digital_World_part1.pdf+Kumar,+K.+Virtual+design+studios:+Solving+learning+problems+in+developing+countries.&cd=1&hl=en&ct=clnk&gl=gh#35.

Kurubacak, G. (2002). Accomplishing access and equity in education: Using the web to design and deliver courses online. *Turkish Online Journal of Distance Education—TOJDE* 3 (4). Retrieved April 12, 2009, from http://tojde.anadolu.edu.tr/tojde8/articles/equityineducation.htm.

Kwapong, O. A. T. F. (2009a). Comparing knowledge and usage of ICT among male and female distance learners of an endowed and deprived area in a developing country in Africa. *Journal of Information Technology* 8, 1–17. Retrieved January 5, 2009, from http://jite.org/documents/Vol8/JITEv8Contents.pdf; http://jite.org/documents/Vol8/JITEv8p001-017Kwapong415.pdf.

Kwapong, O. A. T. F. (2009b). A comparison of ICT knowledge and usage among female distance learners in endowed and deprived communities of a developing country. *E–Learning* 6 (2). www.wwwords.co.uk/ELEA; www.wwwords.co.uk/pdf/validate.asp?j=elea&vol=6&issue=2&year=2009&article=2_Kwapong_ELEA_6_2_web.

Kwapong, O. A. T. F. (2009c). Assessing Internet usage among males and females in an African community. *Indian Journal of Open Learning* 18 (1), 28–43.

Kwapong, O. A. T. F. (2008d). *Education at doorsteps of women—Open and distance learning for empowerment of women.* Booksurge Publishing, South Carolina.

Kwapong, O. A. T. F. (2008a). A case for using open and distance learning (ODL) to widen access to tertiary education for women. *International Journal of Instructional Technology and Distance Learning* 5 (5), 47–59. Retrieved September 28, 2008, from http://itdl.org/Journal/May_08/index.htm; http://itdl.org/Journal/May_08/article04.htm; http://itdl.org/Journal/May_08/May_08.pdf.

Kwapong, O. A. T. F. (2008b). Policy implications for using ICTs for empowerment of rural women in Ghana. *The Turkish Online Journal of Educational Technology—TOJET* 7 (3), 35–45. www.tojet.net/articles/734.htm;

www.tojet.net/volumes/v7i3.pdf; www.tojet.net/results.asp?volume=7&issue=3&year=2008.

Kwapong, O. A. T. F. (2008c). An empirical study of information and communication technology for empowerment of rural women in Ghana. *African Journal of Information and Communication Technology* 4 (3). Retrieved January 28, 2008, from http://epress.lib.uts.edu.au/ojs/index.php/ajict/article/view/E1I1092008009/982.

Kwapong, O A. T. F. (2007). Widening access to tertiary education for women in Ghana through distance education. *Turkish Online Journal of Distance Education—TOJDE* 8 (4), 65–79.

Kyama, R., and J. Waititu (2008). ICT changing the fortunes of rural communities. Retrieved May 19, 2008, from http://www.elearning-africa.com/newsportal/english/news134.php.

Latchem, C., A. Maru, and K. Alluri (2004). Lifelong learning for farmers (L3Farmers) —A report and recommendations to the commonwealth of learning on open and distance lifelong learning for smallholder farmers and agricultural communities. Retrieved April 9, 2009, from www.col.org/progServ/programs/livelihoods/L3farmers/Pages/default.aspx.

Lee, W. O. (2004). Equity and access to education: themes, tensions, and policies. Retrieved March 16, 2009, from http://www.adb.org/Documents/Books/Education_NatlDev_Asia/Equity_Access/default.asp; http://www.adb.org/Documents/Books/Education_NatlDev_Asia/Equity_Access/introduction.pdf; http://www.adb.org/

Documents/Books/Education_NatlDev_Asia/Equity_Access/equity_access.pdf.

Leinonen, J. T., E. Smith, and R. M. Haataja (2006). A manual of possible interventions to improve the situation of women in high-level ICTs in South Africa. Retrieved March 21, 2008, from http://women-in-ict.meraka.csir.co.za/images/b/b5/Manual_print.pdf.

Lindsay, G. (2002). ICTs for open and distance learning: Some experiences and strategies from the commonwealth. Retrieved April 19, from www.col.org/SiteCollectionDocuments/Women%20and%20ICTs.pdf.

Magagula, C. (2002). Evaluation report of the course for distance education policy-makers in Southern Africa. Retrieved April 17, 2009, from www.col.org/resources/publications/consultancies/Pages/2002-03-policySA.aspx.

Mangesi, K. (2007). Survey of ICT in education in Ghana. Retrieved April 6, 2009, from www.infodev.org/en/Publication.354.html.

Maplecroft maps (2006). Information and communication technology: 2006–2008. Retrieved May 11, 2008, from http://forum.maplecroft.com/loadmap?template=map.

May, K. (1994). Women's experiences as distance learners: Access and technology. *The Journal of Distance Education* 9 (1).

McIsaac, M. S., and C. N. Gunawardena (1996). Distance education. In D. H. Jonassen, ed. *Handbook of research for educational communications and technology: a project of the Association for Educational Communications and Technology.* New York: Simon & Schuster Macmillan.

McPherson, M., and M. P. Nunes (2004). The role of tutors as an integral part of online learning support. *European Journal of Open, Distance and E-Learning*. Retrieved May 11, 2009, from www.eurodl.org/?p=archives&year=2004&halfyear=1&article=105.

Mensah, S. K. E., and F. Owusu-Mensah (2002). Priorities and strategies for capacity building in tertiary distance education for human resources development in Ghana. Retrieved April 17, 2009 from http://siteresources. worldbank. org/

Mhehe, E. (2006). Women overcoming barriers to learning by distance at the Open University of Tanzania. *Turkish Online Journal of Distance Education—TOJDE*. Retrieved March 30, 2009, from www.jofde.ca/index.php/jde/article/view/381/271; www.col.org/pcf2/papers/mhehe.pdf.

Mitchell, B., and K. Murugan (2000). The use of public broadcasting in the Caribbean for open/distance learning: Feasibility study report. Retrieved April 23, 2009, from www.col.org/resources/publications/consultancies/Pages/2000-05-publicBroadcast.aspx.

Middlehurst, R., and S. Woodfield (2003). Retrieved April 9, 2009, from www.col.org/resources/publications/consultancies/Pages/2003-10-role.aspx.

Mitra, S. (2008). *An overview of open and distance learning. Retrieved March 8, 2009, from* www.col.org/SiteCollectionDocuments/Manual_for_the_tutors_of_learning_centres_in_open_schools.pdf; http://creativecommons.org/licenses/by-sa/3.0.

Mkoka, C. (2009). ICT projects for African health. Retrieved March 21, 2009, from http://go.worldbank.org/NTWBZ2K4E0; www.scidev.net/en/news/task-force-proposes-ict-projects-for-african-healt.html.

Ministry of Local Government and Rural Development & environment (MLGRD) (2006). Greater Accra, Northern, Upper East Upper West Regions retrieved May 5, 2008, from http://www.ghanadistricts.com/region/?r=1; www.ghanadistricts.com/region/?r=8; www.ghanadistricts.com/region/?r=9; www.ghanadistricts.com/region/?r=6.

MOESS (2009). Educational statistics. Retrieved March 23, 2009, from www.moess.gov.gh/download.htm; www.moess.gov.gh/.

MOESS (2008). Policy evaluation study. Monitoring and Evaluation Unit, PBME Division, Accra.

MOESS (2007a). Ghana National Education Campaign Coalition—Africa education watch. Retrieved May 20, 2009, from www.moess.gov.gh/Ghana@50%20Contemporary%20issues%20on%20Education,%20November%202007.pdf.

MOESS (2007b). Major highlights. Retrieved March 9, 2009, from www.moess.gov.gh/educreform.htm.

Moffatt, S. (1997). Gender issues in teaching information technology courses by distance education. *Distance Education* 18 (2), 369–379.

Tait, A. (2003). Reflections on student support in open and distance learning. *The International Review of Research in Open and Distance Learning* 4 (1). Retrieved May

9, 2009, from www.irrodl.org/index.php/irrodl/article/viewArticle/134/214.

Tait, A. (2000). Planning student support for open and distance learning. *Open Learning 15* (3), 287–299.

Tait, A., and R. Mills (2002). Introduction. In A. Tait and R. Mills (eds.) *Rethinking learner support in distance education: change and continuity in an international context*. London: Routledge.

MTN (2008). Get more with MTN—What's on offer? Retrieved January 29, 2009, from www.mtn.com.gh/.

Nagel, G. (n.d.). Towards access and equity: the education of students with visual impairment in New Zealand. Retrieved April 12, 2009, from www.adb.org/Documents/Books/Education_NatlDev_Asia/Equity_Access/country_groups.pdf.

NCA (2005). National Communications Authority data. Accra, Ghana.

NCTE (2006). Statistics on tertiary education in Ghana: Ministry of Education.

OECD (2004). ICTs and gender-evidence from OECD and non-OECD countries. Retrieved March 21, 2008, from http://go.worldbank.org/ZWPCWFSFV0; www.oecd.org/dataoecd/20/23/31641866.pdf.

Olakunein, F. K., and O. D. Ojo (2006). Distance education as a women empowerment strategy in Africa. *Turkish Online Journal of Distance Education—TOJDE.* Retrieved March

30, 2009, from http://tojde.anadolu.edu.tr/tojde21/pdf/article_13.pdf.

Opoku, R. A. (2004). ICT opportunities in Ghana—A lesson for the government and Ghanaian entrepreneurs. Retrieved March 11, 2009, from www.ghanaweb.com/GhanaHomePage/features/artikel.php?ID=49218.

PCWorld (2008). Ghana likely to exceed targets for telephone penetration. Retrieved April 17, 2009, from www.pcworld.com/businesscenter/article/147145/ghana_likely_to_exceed_targets_for_telephone_penetration.html.

Pecku, N. K. (1998). Survey of current status of distance education in Cameroon. Retrieved April 12, 2009, from www.col.org/resources/publications/consultancies/Pages/1998-02-surveyCameroon.aspx.

Perraton, H. (1997). The cost effectiveness of distance education for primary teacher training. Retrieved May 23, 2009, from www.col.org/resources/publications/consultancies/Pages/1997-costEffective.aspx.

Phillip, A. (1993). Problems for women in distance education at the University of Papua New Guinea. *The Journal of Open and Distance Learning* 8 (1).

Plummer, V. C. (2000). *Women and distance education.* London: Routledge.

Plummer, V. C., ed. (2004). *Gender issues and learning online: Learner support in open, distance and online learning environments.* Oldenburg: Bibliotheks-und Informationssystem der.

Priebe, L. C., L. R. Tamra, and K. W. Low (2008). Exploring the role of distance education in fostering equitable university access for first generation students: A phenomenological survey. *The International Review of Research in Open and Distance Learning* 9 (1).

Prummer, C. V. (2007). Distance education. In B. J. Bank (ed), *Gender and education—An encyclopedia* (Vol. 1). London: Praeger Publishers.

PSDL (2002). The president's special initiative on distance learning at a glance. Retrieved January 12, 2009, from www.ghana.gov.gh/ghana/presidents_special_initiative_distance_learning_glance.jsp.

Pym, F. R. (1992). Women and distance education: a nursing perspective. *Journal of Advanced Nursing*. journals.cs@oxon.blackwellpublishing.com; www.blackwell-synergy.com/doi/abs/10.1111/j.1365-2648.1992.tb01917.x?journalCode=jan.

Rahman, K. M. R., S. Anwar, and S. M. Numan (2008). Enhancing distant learning through e-mail communication: A case of Bou. *Turkish Online Journal of Distance Education—TOJDE* 9 (2). Retrieved March 20, 2008, from http://tojde.anadolu.edu.tr/tojde30/index.htm.

Ramanujam, P. R. (1997). Exploration of strategies to meet the needs of the disabled in India. Retrieved May 12, 2009, from www.col.org/resources/publications/consultancies/Pages/1997-disabledindia.aspx.

Rathore, H. C. S., S. K. Singh, and G. Dubey (1996). Problems of women students in distance education in India. *Indian Journal of Online Learning*. Retrieved March

21, 2009, from http://cemca.org/disted/Rathore_HCS__Singh_S_K__Dubey_G__0004.pdf.

Rawaf, H. S. A., and C. Simmons (1992). Distance higher education for women in Saudi Arabia: Present and proposed. Retrieved March 29, 2009, from www.informaworld.com/smpp/content~content=a739141051~db=all~order=page; www.col.org/SiteCollectionDocuments/Rawaf_Distance.pdf.

Reddy, V. V., and M. Srivastave (2003). ICT and the future of distance education. *Turkish Online Journal of Distance Education—TOJDE* 4 (4).

Rekkedal, T. (1994). Research in distance education—past, present and future. Retrieved December 21, 2006, from www.nettskolen.com/forskning/29/intforsk.htm.

Remer, J. (2008). What we should expect of public education: access and equity meet the thorn of quality. Retrieved April 10, 2009, from www.artsjournal.com/artsed/2008/01/the-author.html.

Roberts, D. (n.d.). *Learner support in South African distance education: A case for action.* University of South Africa, Johannesburg.

Robinson, B. (2008). Using distance education and ICT to improve access, equity and the quality in rural teachers' professional development in western China. *The International Review of Research in Open and Distance Learning* 9 (1).

Rooy, S. V. (2008). Capacity of ODL practitioners in the area of design, development and management of distance education study materials in Lesotho. Retrieved April 9, 2009, from www.col.org/resources/publications/consultancies/Pages/2008-09-05.aspx.

Rumble, G. (2008). Access and equity in distance education. Retrieved April 12, 2009, from *ww.uned.ac.cr/XIVCongreso/memoria/pdf%20expertos/Conferencia%20Greville%20Rumble.pdf.*

Rumble, R., and K. N. Badri (2007). Open schooling for secondary and higher secondary education: Costs and effectiveness in India and Namibia. Retrieved April 9, 2009, from www.col.org/resources/publications/consultancies/Pages/2007-07-openSchl.aspx.

Rwangoga, N. T., and A. P. Baryayetunga (2007). E-government for Uganda: Challenges and opportunities. *International Journal of Computing and ICT Research* 1(1/5), 36–46. www.ijcir.org/volume1-number1/article 5.pdf.

Sales, G., T. Al-Barwani, and S. Miske (2007). Prospects and challenges of an online teacher-training project in Oman. *International Journal of Education and Development Using ICT* 4 (1). Retrieved March 15, 2008, from http://ijedict.dec.uwi.edu/viewarticle.php?id=408&layout=html.

Schmieder, E. J. (2008). Communication: The tool to interact with and control your online classroom environment. *International Journal of Instructional Technology and Distance Learning* 5 (3).

Scollins-Mantha, B. (2008). Cultivating social presence in the online learning classroom: A literature review with recommendations for practice. *International Journal of Instructional Technology and Distance Learning* 5 (3).

Siaciwena, R. (2000). Case studies of non-formal education by distance and open learning. Retrieved April 18, 2009, from www.col.org/resources/publications/consultancies/Pages/2000-nonFormalEdu.aspx.

Som, N. (2003). Retrieved April 23, 2009, from www.cemca.org/e-learn.htm.

South Africa (2008). All Africa.com: North West women to further ICT skills. Retrieved March 20, 2008, from http://allafrica.com/stories/200709110469.html.

Spencer, B. (1994). Removing barriers and enhancing openness: Distance education as social adult education. *Journal of Distance Education* 10 (2).

Spodick, E. F. (1996). The evolution of distance learning. Retrieved April 20, 2009, from http://en.wikipedia.org/wiki/Distance_learning; www.digitalschool.net/edu/DL_history_mJeffries.html; http://en.wikipedia.org/wiki/Distance_learning.

Spronk, B. (1990). Gender in distance education. *The Journal of Distance Education* 5 (2), 1–2.

Ssewanyana, J. K. (2007). ICT access and poverty in Uganda. *International Journal of Computing and ICT Research* 1 (2/2), 10–19. www.ijcir.org/volume1-number2/article 2.pdf.

Swale, C. (1999). The facilitation of the transfer of learning materials. Retrieved April 12, 2009, from www.col.org/SiteCollectionDocuments/transmanual99.pdf.

Tigo (n.d.). About Tigo. Retrieved April 9, 2009, from www.tigo.com.gh/internal.jsp?article_id=art0908219370025.

Thomas, J. (2001). Audio for distance education and open learning: a practical guide for planners and producers. Retrieved April 9, 2009, from www.col.org/resources/publications/operational/Pages/audioDEOL.aspx.

Thorpe, M. (2002). Rethinking learner support: the challenge of on-line learning. *Open Learning 17* (2), 105–120.

Touré, H. I. (2007). Current situation in Africa. Retrieved March 20, 2009, from www.itu.int/ITU-D/connect/africa/2007/bgdmaterial/chap1-5.html.

Tripathi, P., and S. Mukerji (2008). Access and equity to education in India through synergy of conventional and ODL systems: A step towards democratization of education. Retrieved May 20, 2009, from www.distanceandaccesstoeducation.org/contents/OP2008-IGNOU.pdf.

UMPA (2003). Council of Australian Postgraduate Associations. Retrieved April 23, 2009, from www.umpa.unimelb.edu.au/about/policy-pdf/501Accessandequity.pdf.

UNESCO (2000). The six EFA goals. Retrieved March 9, 2009, from http://portal.unesco.org/education/en/ev.php-URL_ID=43811&URL_DO=DO_TOPIC&URL_SECTION=201.html.

UNESCO (2002). Open and distance learning—Trends, policy and strategy considerations. Retrieved May 11, 2007, from http://unesdoc.unesco.org/images/0012/001284/128463e.pdf.

UNESCO (2003). Towards a more equitable information society: How and why of gender mainstreaming. Retrieved March 21, 2008, from http://portal.unesco.org/ci/en/file_download.php/250561f24133814c18284feedc30bb5egender_issues.pdf.

UNESCO (2004). Schoolnet toolkit. Retrieved April 9, 2009, from www.unescobkk.org/education/ict/v2/info.asp?id=16282.

UNESCO (2006). Equity, access and quality—Improving transparency in the targeting of pro-poor incentives. Retrieved April 9, 2009, from www.acenet.edu/bookstore/pdf/Gender_Equity_6_23.pdf; www.iiep.unesco.org/?id=725&.

UNESCO (2008). Country profile commissioned for the EFA Global Monitoring Report 2008, Education for All by 2015: will we make it? Retrieved May 11, 2009, from www.unesco.org/education/efa/ed_for_all/dakfram_eng.shtml.

UNISA (2007). A further update and analysis of 2007 registration statistics. Department of Information and Strategic Analysis.

UEW (2006). Students' Statistics. University of Education, Winneba.

UG (2007). Report of the visitation panel to the University of Ghana. Retrieved April 9, 2009, from www.col.org/resources/publications/consultancies/Pages/2007-07-openSchl.aspx.

Vetinfonet (n.d.). Access and equity—Questions and answers: What is access and equity? Retrieved March 14, 2009, from http://vetinfonet.det.wa.edu.au/AccessEquity/faq.aspx?menu=5&menuItem=1#What%20is%20A%20&%20E.

Vodaphone (2009). Homepage. Retrieved March 9, 2009, from www.vodafone.com.gh/.

Wall, L. (2004). Women, distance education and solitude: a feminist postmodern narrative of women's responses to learning in solitude. M.A. thesis submitted to Athabasca University, Alberta, May 2004. Retrieved September 1, 2007, from http://auspace.athabascau.ca:8080/dspace/bitstream/2149/568/1/wall.pdf.

Wang, C. and Z. Liu (n.d.). Distance education: basic resources guide. Retrieved September 1, 2007, from www.emeraldinsight.com/Insight/ViewContentServlet?Filename=Published/EmeraldFullTextArticle/Articles/1710220302.html.

Williams, R. (2000). Diffusion of appropriate educational technology in open and distance learning in developing commonwealth countries. Retrieved April 12, 2009, from www.col.org/resources/publications/consultancies/Pages/2000-08-appTech.aspx.

World Bank (2009). Using GPS technology to improve agricultural productivity in Senegal. Retrieved March 22, 2009, from http://web.worldbank.org/WBSITE/EXTERNAL/COUNTRIES/AFRICAEXT/0,,contentMDK:22086471~menuPK:258649~pagePK:2865106~piPK:2865128~theSitePK:258644,00.html.

Women'snet (2005). Mainstreaming ICTs Africa lives the information society—A handbook for development practitioners. Retrieved March 21, 2008, from Africahttp://www.womensnet.org.za/publications/mainstreaming_ICTs/womensnet6.pdf.

Wong, A. L. (2008). Cross-cultural delivery of e-learning programs: Perspectives from Hong Kong. *Turkish Online Journal of Distance Education—TOJDE* 9 (2/1).

World Bank (2007). *The Little Data Book on Information and Communication Technology.* World Bank.

World Bank Ghana (2008). Country unit www. Retrieved June 9, 2009, from http://web.worldbank.org/WBSITE/EXTERNAL/DATASTATISTICS/0,,contentMDK:20485916~menuPK:1297819~pagePK:64133150~piPK:64133175~theSitePK:239419,00.html.

Yiwan, L., and Q. Wei. (2008). How to realize social fairness and equality through distance and open learning? Retrieved June 2, 2009, from www.distanceandaccesstoeducation.org/contents/OP2008-Li_Yawan.pdf.

Yousuf, I. M., M. N. Anwar, and M. Sarwar (2008). Perceptions of course coordinators and course writers for developing distance learning material. *Turkish Online Journal of Distance Education—TOJDE* 9 (2/6).

Zain (2009). What makes Zain different. Retrieved March 3, 2009, from www.gh.zain.com/en/.